The Church of Scientology

The Church of Scientology

J. Gordon Melton

STUDIES IN CONTEMPORARY RELIGIONS

Massimo Introvigne, Series Editor

Signature Books
in cooperation with CESNUR
(Center for Studies on New Religions)

Grateful acknowledgement is made to the following organizations: to L. Ron Hubbard Library for permission to reproduce the photograph of L. Ron Hubbard; to Religious
Technology Center for permission to reproduce the photograph of David Miscavige; to the Church of Scientology
International for photographs originally appearing in its
publications; and to the Association for Better Living and
Education for photographs originally appearing in its
publications and/or its licensed social betterment
programs.

Cover design by Ron Stucki

© 2000 Elle Di Ci, Leumann (Torino), Italy.

This edition is published by arrangement with the copyright holder.

Published in the United States of America by Signature
Books. Signature Books is a registered trademark of
Signature Books, Inc.

LIBRARY OF CONGRESS CATALOGING-IN-PUBLICATION DATA
Melton, J. Gordon.
    [Chiesa di Scientology. English]
    The Church of Scientology / by J. Gordon Melton.
        p.   cm. — (Studies in contemporary religions ; 1)
    Includes bibliographical references.
    ISBN 1-56085-139-2 (pbk.)
      1. Scientology. I. Title. II. Series.

    BP605.S2 M46 2000
    299'.936—dc21

                                        99-086785

Contents

1.

Birth of a Religion

As the twenty-first century opens, the Church of Scientology[1] has emerged as one major focus of the ongoing controversy on new religions and their role in the rise of religious pluralism in the West. The teachings of founder L. Ron Hubbard enjoyed some immediate success with the public following their initial appearance in 1950, but one could have hardly predicted Scientology's meteoric rise or its history of public conflict from its modest beginning. The controversy over Scientology has extended at times to almost every aspect of the church and its founder, and while those issues have been largely resolved in North America, the very status of Scientology as a religion continues to be seriously questioned in some quarters and has been the subject of multiple court cases. True, it has been recognized as a religion in many countries of the world, including the United States; but opposition continues in some quarters. In the modest space allowed, this essay cannot cover every point at issue, but does attempt to provide (1) an overview of the life of L. Ron Hubbard anchored by the generally agreed upon facts; (2) an introduction to the church's beliefs, practices, and organization; and (3) a summary of the major points of the controversy.

THE FOUNDER

Lafayette Ronald Hubbard (1911-1986) began life in the rural Midwest, born in Tilden, Nebraska, to U.S. naval officer Harry Ross Hubbard and Ledora May Waterbury.[2] Six months after his birth, the family moved from Nebraska to Oklahoma, then settled for a time in Montana, eventually establishing itself on a ranch near Helena. The land was still frontier country, and the youthful Hubbard learned to be at home on a horse. Befriended by the local Blackfoot Indians, he was made a blood brother at the age of six.[3] After some five years, the family was on the move again, and in October 1923 headed for Washington, D.C. Memorable on the trip East to the twelve-year-old Hubbard was a meeting with U.S. Navy commander Joseph "Snake" Thompson. Over the next couple of months, Thompson, a student of Sigmund Freud, introduced Hubbard to the inner workings of the mind being explored by depth psychology, and the youth felt encouraged to begin his own independent explorations.[4]

In March 1925 Hubbard returned to the family homestead in Montana and was still residing there when, in the summer of 1927, he made his first excursion to foreign lands, a summer trip that included brief stops in Hawaii, Japan, China (including Hong Kong), the Philippines, and finally Guam, where he taught school with the native Chamorros for several weeks. Returning for a last year at Helena High School, he got a start on his writing career with articles submitted to the school newspaper (including stories of his summer travels). He also became an editor for the newspaper. In 1928 he returned to the Orient for a longer visit. For fourteen months he journeyed around China (including at least one inland trip), Japan, the Philippines, and Indonesia, and for a period served as helmsman and supercargo aboard a twin-masted coastal schooner. In September 1929 he returned to finish his high school education at Swavely Prep School in Manassas, Virginia, (February 1930) and Woodward School for Boys in Washington, D.C. (June 1930).

After graduating from Woodward, in the fall of 1930 he enrolled at George Washington University (GWU). He led a varied student life that included singing and script-writing on the local radio station, writing dramas, and taking a course in subatomic physics. As flying captured the imagination of the nation, Hubbard became an accomplished pilot and president of the GWU Flying Club. In fact, his flying enthusiasm occasioned his first sale of a piece of writing, a nonfiction article, "Tailwind Willies," to *Sportsman Pilot* (Jan. 1932). He soon followed it with his first published fiction stories, "Tah" (*The University Hatchet,* Feb. 1932) and "Grounded" (*The University Hatchet,* Apr. 1932). As the school year closed, he won the GWU Literary Award for his one-act play "The God Smiles."

While writing had clearly manifested as Hubbard's primary talent, his early travels as a teen also prepared him for what was to be a significant sub-theme—exploring. He was still in his early twenties when in 1932 he organized and led more than fifty students on a two-and-a-half month tour of the Caribbean aboard a 200-foot, four-masted schooner. Amid the fun of the trip, a scientific team that joined the cruise gathered a selection of tropical plants and animals later deposited at the University of Michigan. Soon after the trip, Hubbard left again for the West Indies to work on a mineralogical survey in the new American territory of Puerto Rico.

Hubbard left the university after only two years, and in 1933 married. It was time to settle down and make a living, and the popular pulp magazines provided employment. His first story, "The Green God," appeared in *Thrilling Adventures* in February 1934. He wrote rapidly (a talent his fellow authors would always envy) and turned out story after story that frequently appeared under a variety of imaginative pen names (Winchester Remington Colt, Bernard Hubbel, René Lafayette, Scott Morgan, Kurt von Rachen, and John Seabrook). It was a common practice for pulps to rely upon a few valued writers while appearing to draw from a much larger stable of writers than they actually possessed.

Through the mid-1930s, Hubbard produced many different kinds of stories for the pulps, from westerns to supernatural fantasy. He also turned out his first novel, *Buckskin Brigades*, in 1937. That same year Columbia Pictures purchased the film rights to a second novel, *Murder at Pirate Castle*, and Hubbard moved to Hollywood for a few months to work on the screenplay. His book was seen on the big screen as the serial *Secret of Treasure Island*. He remained in California to work on two additional serials produced by Columbia, *The Mysterious Pilot* and *The Adventures of Wild Bill Hickok*, and on *The Spider Returns*, an early superhero adventure done by Warner Brothers.

Shortly after his return to New York from the West Coast, he came into touch with the publishers of *Astounding Science Fiction*. Though continuing to write in other genres, he would find his greatest fame in science fiction (and the related fields of fantasy and horror) and would become one of the noteworthy voices in that primal generation that created the field as it is known today. Over the next few years he would become friends with *Astounding*'s editor, John W. Campbell, Jr., for whom he produced an initial story, "The Dangerous Dimension," for the July

1938 issue. He also became a regular contributor to Campbell's fantasy magazine, *Unknown,* for which Hubbard produced one of his greatest pieces of fiction, *Fear,* originally published in the June 1940 issue. He quickly established himself in the community of writers of popular fiction, a fact signaled in 1935 by his election as president of the New York chapter of the American Fiction Guild. Increasingly, during his spare time, he was sought out by aspiring writers looking for words of advice, encouragement, and assistance.

THE DISRUPTION OF WAR

Though writing consumed his time, Hubbard never lost his adventurous spirit, and, with war already a reality in Europe, he found new uses for his interests. In 1940 he was elected a member of the Explorers Club and in June sailed under its banner as head of the Alaskan Radio Experimental Expedition. His group charted the coastline north of Seattle to the Alaskan panhandle for the U.S. Navy Hydrographic Office, experimented with radio directional finding, and included some anthropological observations of the Native American peoples of the region. As the expedition was drawing to a close, in December the U.S. Bureau of Marine Inspection and Navigation awarded him a "Master of Steam and Motor Vessels" license. Three months later he received his "Master of Sail Vessels" license for any ocean.[5]

Hubbard was commissioned as a lieutenant (junior grade) in the U.S. Naval Reserve in late June. He was called to active duty following the attack on Pearl Harbor and ordered to the Philippines. With the subsequent Japanese takeover of the Philippines, he began his wartime service with naval intelligence in Australia. His later posts during the war included command of convoy escort YP 422 in

Boston; command of the sub chaser PC 815 in the North
Pacific; and navigation officer aboard the *USS Algol*. It appears that PC 815 did engage and sink a Japanese subma-
rine off the Oregon coast, a fact only recently substantiated
because of the American government's reluctance to admit
that the Japanese were in fact operating off America's Pacific Coast during the war. He spent the last months of the
war at Oak Knoll Naval Hospital in Oakland, California.[6]
While recovering, he had time to give consideration to the
larger questions of the nature of the human mind and to
help some of his fellow patients who had not survived the
war in the best of mental health. It appears that the months
in Oak Knoll provided an occasion during which the earlier ruminations on the human problem were intensified
and a period of more systematic consideration of the human condition was launched.[7]

Following his release from active duty in February
1946, Hubbard to all outward appearances returned to his
prewar life. His first marriage having ended, he married
again and picked up his writing career. He churned out a
number of short stories, among the most enduring being
the "Ole Doc Methuselah" series, a collection of seven
short stories which originally appeared in *Astounding Science Fiction* under Hubbard's pen name René Lafayette and
more recently gathered and published as a single volume.
The stories centered upon a 700-year-old Soldier of Light
who traveled throughout the galaxy performing astonish-
ing medical feats and, contrary to standard professional
ethics, involving himself in interesting areas of interplane-
tary politics.

Immediately after the war, in December 1945, but while
still a commissioned officer and on active duty, Hubbard
became involved in one of the most intriguing episodes in

his long life, participation in the activities of the Ordo Templi Orientis. The OTO is a ritual magic group, then headed by the aging Aleister Crowley (1875-1947), the famous and somewhat notorious occultist. It practiced what it saw as real magick (as opposed to stage magic); the secret ritual of the group involved the use of sex to raise magical energies. After World War II, the Agape Lodge of the OTO was opened in Pasadena, California, and one John W. (Jack) Parsons (1914-52), an explosives expert and key man at the California Institute of Technology, emerged as a leader of the small group. Soon after his discharge from Oak Knoll, Hubbard showed up at the Pasadena OTO headquarters.

According to accounts published by the OTO, Parsons developed an immediate liking for Hubbard and invited him to participate in the OTO work, though Hubbard refused to become a member. Even though Hubbard was not properly initiated, he assisted Parsons on several magical operations in what he would later claim was in fulfillment of his military intelligence function.[8] For whatever reason, early in 1946 Parsons and Hubbard had a parting of the ways. Parsons claimed that Hubbard had persuaded him to sell the property of the Agape Lodge, after which Hubbard, along with Parsons's sister-in-law Betty, allegedly absconded with the money. Hubbard reappeared on a newly purchased yacht off the Florida coast. Parsons pursued him, and on 5 July 1946 a confrontation occurred. Hubbard had sailed at 5:00 p.m. At 8:00 p.m., Parsons performed a full magical invocation to "Bartzabel." Coincidentally, a sudden squall struck the yacht, ripped the sails, and forced Hubbard to port, where Parsons was able to recover at least a small percentage of the money.

Hubbard's account (and that of the present-day Church of Scientology) denies any attachment to the OTO. Rather, Hubbard claimed that in his capacity as a U.S. intelligence officer, he was sent to scrutinize Parsons and the lodge. The building that served as the lodge's headquarters also housed a number of nuclear physicists living there while working at Cal Tech (and these physicists were among sixty-four later dismissed from government service as security risks). Hubbard asserted that, due to his efforts, the headquarters was torn down, a girl rescued from the group, and the group ultimately destroyed.

Both stories stand and, in fact, may be genuine perceptions of the events since Hubbard obviously would not make any undercover "investigative" operation known to Parsons. These events also appear to be the source of charges that Hubbard based Scientology's teachings in part on Crowley's. It should be noted that, whatever happened during Hubbard's association with Parsons, the teachings of the Church of Scientology are at wide variance with those of Crowley and that the practices of the church show no direct OTO influence.[9]

Quite apart from the OTO, however, in light of the later emergence of the Dianetics movement and the Church of Scientology, it is obvious that Hubbard was spending the greater part of his energies during these postwar years on his personal research aimed at finding a technology of the human mind. He was synthesizing all he had read and learned into what would be a novel approach to the problem.[10] He first compiled his thoughts in 1948 into a short book, *The Original Thesis,*[11] which he circulated privately. It contained his basic conclusions concerning the nature of human aberrations and his early ideas about handling them through the counseling technique called auditing.

Knowledge of his new ideas within his friendship network led to his initial published articles on Dianetics, "Terra Incognita: The Mind," in *The Explorers Club Journal* (Winter/Spring 1948/1950) and the far more influential one in *Astounding Science Fiction.*[12]

Favorable response to *The Original Thesis* led to his expanding it into a more substantial volume, *Dianetics: The Modern Science of Mental Health,*[13] whose publication on 9 May 1950 is considered by Scientologists a seminal event of the century. The appearance of *Dianetics* has, they believe, ushered in a new era of hope for humankind. The next month it hit the *New York Times* bestseller list and there remained for the rest of the year. Concurrently, Hubbard founded the Hubbard Dianetic Research Foundation in Elizabeth, New Jersey, where he held classes to train people as auditors. He also toured the country lecturing on the principles presented in the book.

Overnight Hubbard had become the leader of a popular movement that was growing faster than anyone had expected. Above and beyond responding to people who wanted to know more or wished to be audited, he faced an immediate need to provide guidelines for auditors (from the Latin *audire,* "to listen"). People were purchasing his book and auditing each other with the instructions they found in its pages. Hubbard launched a series of training lectures and had the notes from his "Professional Course" (Nov. 1950) transcribed and published.

During 1951 he intensified efforts to offer direction to the growing movement. He increased the number of public lectures, but concentrated teaching time on the training of auditors. He also found time to write two important new texts—*Science of Survival*[14] and *Self-Analysis.*[15] Possibly the most important addition to Dianetics during the year,

however, came with the incorporation of the electropsychometer or E-meter. Developed by Volney Matheson, following Hubbard's designs, the small device measures emotional reactions to a tiny electrical current. To Scientologists, the changes in the E-meter measure changes in the
mind and tell what the pre-Clear's mind is doing when the
pre-Clear is induced to think of something, though its indi-
cations must be interpreted by a trained auditor. (For more
on these terms, see Chapter 2.) The E- meter gave Scientology a means of quantifying the counseling experience (a
possibility about which most psychotherapists are exreme-
ly skeptical).[16]

Not everyone inspired by their reading of *Dianetics*
came into association with the foundation. A number of organizations, each with its own variation on Hubbard's
ideas and practices, arose. At the same time Hubbard's own
investigations brought him up against the phenomenon of
past lives. Through the first half of 1951, the subject of reincarnation became a matter of intense debate on the
board, and in July some members of the board sought to
pass a resolution banning the entire subject.[17] Most notable among those supporting the resolution were John
Campbell, who had supported Hubbard since the publication of the Dianetics article in his magazine, and Dr. Joseph
Winter, a physician who had written a book on Dianetics
and who had hoped to see Dianetics eventually accepted by
his physician colleagues.[18] With the changing personnel,
his organization went through various corporate changes,
and in 1952 Hubbard founded the Hubbard Association of
Scientologists (later adding the word International) as a
more permanent corporate structure. He also launched the
Journal of Scientology to keep followers abreast of the growing movement and issued a regular series of technical pub-

lications to further the auditors' training and keep them abreast of the latest developments.

The appearance of the term Scientology indicated the emergence of a distinct new emphasis in the movement Hubbard had founded. Dianetics concentrated on the mind, believed to be the mechanism which receives, records, and stores images of experiences. In several years since the publication of *Dianetics,* amid the time-consuming task of training auditors, Hubbard shifted his attention away from the mind itself to the entity observing the images that the mind was storing. That entity—he called it a thetan, from the Greek letter *theta,* for thought or life— closely resembled what other religions had called the soul or spirit. Hubbard was clearly venturing into theological realms, inspired somewhat by Eastern religious perspectives, especially manifest in his acceptance of past lives.

The development of a more comprehensive understanding of the human being that included consideration of humanity's place in the cosmos suggested the emergence of Scientology into the field of religion. By 1954 students of Dianetics and Scientology were already acknowledging that Scientology functioned for them as their religion. Thus it came as no surprise when, in February 1954, some of Hubbard's followers, operating independently of him but clearly with his blessing, organized the first local Church of Scientology.[19]

While the movement was expanding rapidly in the United States, Dianetics was also finding an audience overseas. In late 1952, when Hubbard first traveled to England, he found a group of people already using his book. And as he was opening the training center in London, he discovered that there were similar responses to his teachings throughout the English speaking world, from Ireland to

Australia to South Africa. There were eager students even in far off Israel, and the second local Church of Scientology was opened neither in Chicago nor New York, but in Auckland, New Zealand.

In March 1955, Hubbard moved east where the Founding Church of Scientology in Washington, D.C., was opened, and he assumed duties as its executive director. From that post, he began the process of developing the church's administration procedures. He also formed a distribution center to oversee the publication and dissemination of Dianetics/Scientology literature (the seed of what is now Bridge Publications).

The international spread of Scientology during the last half of the 1950s was capped by the opening of churches in Johannesburg, South Africa (1957), and Paris, France (1959), the first in a non-English-speaking country. World headquarters was moved to England where Saint Hill, a rural estate, had been purchased at East Grinstead, Sussex. Hubbard would live there for the next seven years. However, before he really settled in, he finished off the decade with a round-the-world tour highlighted by stops in Greece and India, and a series of lectures in Melbourne and London. The new decade began on an optimistic note, but storm clouds had gathered and a deluge was about to burst upon the young church.

ENCOUNTERING THE POWERS THAT BE

When Hubbard first circulated his ideas on the mind, its operation, and the implications for medicine, he offered his findings to both the American Psychiatric Association and the American Medical Association. He found them uninterested.[20] They declined to take Dianetics seriously. Hubbard's approach to the mind did not connect with the state of psychiatry at the time, and the American Medical Association looked askance at nonprofessionals they considered were attempting to enter their ranks with magic bullets. They had a long history of examining similar claims only to label them worthless. As a matter of fact, once Hubbard published Dianetics, he found no less a person than Dr. Morris Fishbein, well-known for his exposés of quack medicine, dismissing his book.

With the opening of the Founding Church of Scientology in Washington, D.C., the stage was set for further confrontation. Washington was the headquarters of the Food and Drug Administration (FDA), the federal agency charged with preserving the quality of food and drugs. Although Dianetics as presented in 1950 did not particularly interest them, the introduction of the E-meter with accompanying claims of marked improvement resulting from auditing did attract their attention. Here was something to which possibly unwarranted medical claims were being attached. They began an investigation.

The FDA attention had not arisen in a vacuum, however. As additional congregations of the church were founded, each received its tax-exempt status almost as a matter of routine. However, in 1958 the Internal Revenue Service began to call that status into question. The Church of Scientology did not look like a traditional church, and the language it used to describe its activities was unfamiliar. The initial withdrawal of tax-exempt status (with a resultant demand for back taxes) started a string of appeals, investigations, and litigation that would last for a quarter of a century, the longest set of related litigations in the agency's history.

The questioning of the church's status as a religion (the only long-term grounds for withdrawal of tax exemption) would have dramatic effects. It would lead to the circulation of numerous memos to other government agencies and no doubt lay behind actions that at first glance appeared to be completely unrelated to tax issues. Thus it was that on 4 January 1963 deputized agents of the FDA moved into the Founding Church of Scientology and seized all of the E-meters and thousands of pieces of church literature. It would take eight years for the issue to be resolved in the courts, which would eventually declare the E-meter a legitimate religious artifact and order the return of the Scientology literature.

The circulation of material relative to the IRS action was also used to support the actions of the British and Australian governments. As early as October 1962, psychiatrist E. Cunningham Dax, the chair of the Mental Health Authority in the State of Victoria, recommended the curbing of Scientology, in part by banning its advertisements. He found allies in Labor Minister J. W. Galbally and Kevin Anderson, Q.C. The latter prepared a lengthy report that led the government of Victoria, Australia, in 1965 to pass the Psychological Practices Act that prohibited the practice of Scientology, the use of its name, and the dissemination of its teachings. Western Australia and South Australia soon followed suit. At the beginning of 1969, Scientology churches in Melbourne, Sydney, Perth, and Adelaide reorganized as the Church of the New Faith to pursue their cause. The first step in reversing the legislation occurred in 1969 when the High Court of Western Australia ruled the ban illegal. The law was formally repealed in Western Australia and South Australia in 1973, but it would take almost two decades to reverse all of the negative legislation.[21] The law in Victoria was repealed in 1982, and the following year the High Court of Australia in a unanimous decision ruled that the Church of Scientology (still operating as the Church of the New Faith) was undoubtedly a religion and deserving of tax exemption. The final ruling addressed a number of challenges alleged against the church's religious status and dismissed them. Over the next several years, the tax exempt status of the church was granted in the various states of Australia.[22]

In 1968 the United Kingdom moved against the church, which had expanded its facilities at East Grinstead to include an advanced training center. The health minister barred the entry of non-citizens coming into England specifically to study or work at Saint Hill. A subsequent inquiry into the situation by Sir John Foster recommended a lifting of the ban in 1971; however, it was not acted upon until 1980.[23]

The public controversy over Scientology through the 1960s led to extensive newspaper coverage and finally to a set of books that highlighted the charges being made against the church—George Malko's *Scientology, the Now Religion* (1970), Paulette Cooper's *The Scandal of Scientology* (1971), and Robert Kaufmann's *Inside Scientology* (1972).[24] A more sympathetic treatment appeared in Omar Garrison's *The Hidden History of Scientology* (1974).[25] Church leaders were especially offended by Cooper's work, and favorably settled a major libel case against her.

In 1966, in order to cordon off the attacks on Scientology to some degree and prevent them from interfering with the central activities of counseling and training, the church established the Guardian's Office. It was assigned the mission of protecting the church against outside attacks and ensuring that the organization moved ahead according to the policies laid down in the writings of its founder. The Guardian's Office was designed to handle the obstacles (primarily legal and public relations) to the church's growth. In isolating the rest of the church from any disturbances, theoretically, the day-to-day work of teaching and auditing could continue smoothly. As the number of issues placed on its agenda grew, especially with the addition of the "anti-cult" agitation in the 1970s, the Guardian's Office developed an activist stance. It eventually would oversee an extensive program of intelligence gathering, infiltration of organizations seen as enemies, and the spread of information which it hoped would disrupt actions being taken against the church (black propaganda). Unfortunately, the small group running the Guardian's Office, quite apart from the awareness of the rest of the church's leadership and membership, began to see itself above the laws of both the church and the state. In the end, this group and their operatives committed a number of morally questionable and even illegal acts. It is significant that the majority of accusations against the church refer to actions taken by the Guardian's Office in the 1970s.

The same year that the Guardian's Office was founded, Hubbard resigned all official administrative positions with the church, most notably his post as executive director and his membership on the board of directors. He was given the title "Founder" and withdrew to continue his development of Scientology and to write. He, of course, retained a number of significant ties to the church. His Scientology writings had attained the status of scripture; and as he completed new materials for the church, they were regularly incorporated into its curriculum. He owned the copyrights to all his writings, and received royalties on their sales. More importantly, he remained and remains the source of the spiritual practices and doctrines of the religion, and retained the loyalty of the leadership who regularly looked to him for continued guidance and direction.[26]

Hubbard's turning over the reins of the church to others actually coincided with a significant redirection of his concerns. Through the mid-1960s, he had authored a set of books laying out the overall perspective of the church, had spoken and written extensively on the process of Dianetic and Scientology training, had outlined the church's internal structure, and had created the organizational flow chart now utilized in all church centers. All of this foundational work reached a culminating point in 1965 with the publication of *The Bridge to Freedom,* the "Classification and Gradation Chart" that outlines the steps to be followed by church members as they pursue their study of Scientology. The chart succinctly summarizes the results of all of the development and experimentation that had been conducted since the founding of the Hubbard Dianetics Research Foundation fifteen years previously. While further additions and adjustments would be made over the years, the program for reaching the state of Clear and beginning the process of becoming an Operating Thetan was essentially and clearly delineated.

With the basics completed, Hubbard could turn the movement over to the leaders he had trained and redirect the greater part of his energies to a more complete elucidation of the advanced levels of training. To accomplish this task, in 1967 a new church unit was established, the Sea Organization or Sea Org. The Sea Org was located aboard three ships, the *Diana,* the *Athena,* and the *Apollo,* with the latter serving as the flag ship. Membership was drawn from among the most dedicated of church members. Unlike

Hubbard, the average Sea Org member had no experience as a sailor, and the running of the ships had to be learned from scratch.

Soon after the Sea Org was founded, actually less than a month, Hubbard announced that he had discovered an important breakthrough, the means of erasing those mental factors which stand in the way of peace and toleration for humankind. The material he was releasing to the advanced members would constitute the substance of OT III, a new level on the upper end of the Bridge to Freedom.[27] The release of the materials necessarily involved the training of people who not only had mastered the new levels but who were prepared to teach it. As the teaching spread beyond the ships, those who formerly resided on the ship were reassigned to staff the several Advanced Organizations where the OT teachings would be disseminated to the church.

The Sea Org has attained somewhat of a mythical character among Scientologists. Many are the stories of the hundreds of people who spent time aboard the ships, and those who remain in the church value their opportunity to have been among the chosen few. At the same time, some who left the ships reported bad experiences that eventually provided the church's detractors with scandalous material. In fact, life aboard the Sea Org was a strenuous test of commitment and loyalty to Hubbard and Scientology. Notwithstanding the negative reports, the Sea Org has grown from just those few aboard the ships in the beginning years to more than 6,000 members today.

Life aboard the ships came to an end in 1975. On the one hand, the work for which the Sea Org was created had been completed and the emphasis had once again shifted from the discovery and outlining of the advanced grades to the actual delivery of them to the church membership.

Church staff from around the world had been brought on board to learn of the developments, but the ships' facilities were proving inadequate to handle the flow. On the other hand, various governments around the world were reacting to the negative information about the church generated through several international government agencies. These reports, later shown to have been fabricated, created incidents in some ports where the ships were berthed. Both factors led to the shifting of the Sea Organization to the new Flag Land Base established in Florida.

Quietly, through 1975, the church acquired various properties in downtown Clearwater, Florida, a sleepy resort community whose downtown was going through a period of economic decline. Primary purchases included the Fort Harrison Hotel and the former Bank of Clearwater building. The move of the personnel from the ship into their new facilities on land was marred by intense local reaction to the purchase of the property that had occurred through a third party. Suddenly, city fathers became aware that the town was to become the new headquarters of the church. The Scientologists' attempts to settle in their new home were not helped by the attacks of a local radio station comparing the church to a mafia group and other people simply opposed to the church. In retaliation, a few members of the Guardian's Office attempted some "dirty tricks" against several of the antagonists. When their schemes were uncovered, a decade-long war was set off between the church and its local critics.

The actions of the Guardian's Office in Clearwater, as reprehensible as they were, were overshadowed by the massive disclosure of its activities following the 8 July 1977 raid on the churches in Washington, D.C., and Los Angeles. These raids came a week after a former operative with the Guardian's Office who had been involved in an extensive infiltration operation into various government offices in Washington surrendered to the FBI and told his story. As the full account of what had occurred was uncovered, it read like a Cold War spy novel. It appears that several years after the Guardian's Office was established, a plan was put in place to gather material from the files of various government agencies including the Internal Revenue Service and the Federal Bureau of Investigation. The object was two-fold. In part, it supported the church's attempt to clear government files of what it considered false material about Hubbard and Scientology. Through the 1970s the church filed a variety of Freedom of Information requests in order to locate material which was informing government attitudes toward the church and which was being circulated overseas and causing problems in other countries. Frustrated at times by agencies unwilling to surrender copies of their files, these Guardian's Office staff felt justified in locating and copying them. However, they also had a second, less justified, purpose. It appears that agents began to gather files on various potential enemies of the church and planned to use the information to embarrass, smear, or otherwise render them harmless.

As a result of the raids, the seized files, some 48,000 documents, were made public and eleven officials and agents of the Guardian's Office were indicted. Included were Jane Kember, the international head of the office, and Hubbard's wife Mary Sue. In the end, the actual crimes for which they were convicted were relatively minor, and the sentences, handed down in December 1979, ranged between four and five years in prison with additional fines of $10,000. Far beyond the legal penalties, however, the actions of the Guardian's Office opened the church to broad

censure from both religious and secular leaders who questioned the morality of the church's allowing the gathering
and use of confidential files. It must be said in the church's
defense, however, that following the convictions, the church
stripped the eleven of all offices in the church, and those
later found to have had some role in aiding or covering
their actions were either dismissed from their position and/
or expelled from the church. The incident became a moment of great soul searching for the remaining Scientology
leadership and resulted in a major international reorganization. Among the first acts, the leadership of the Sea Org
disbanded the Guardian's Office.

THE CHURCH OF SCIENTOLOGY INTERNATIONAL

The disclosures of the activities of the Guardian's Office
created a severe crisis. Public access to the seized files provided a basis for a series of civil lawsuits (though most of
these would ultimately be rebuffed). At the same time, the
bad publicity also created problems for the public image of
the church. Thus, even as the trial proceeded, internal
changes were initiated. Among the leaders in the efforts to
reform the church, with Hubbard's sanction, was David
Miscavige, a relatively young leader who had emerged in the
Sea Org. House cleaning began with those convicted in the
court case, but soon led to the demotion of other officials in
the Guardian's Office and eventually to the discontinuance
of the office itself. Through 1980 and into 1981, a number
of personnel shifts occurred, followed by a significant revamping of the church's structure at the highest levels.[28]
That revamping included consideration of the future of the
copyrights of Hubbard's books and the church's trademarks.

    Reorganization resulted in the birth of two key corpo-
rate entities. First, in 1981 the individual churches and

organizations of Scientology were realigned with a new mother church structure, the Church of Scientology International, that now oversees the expansion of Scientology around the world, guides local churches in the application of the teachings (i.e., the technology), and has assumed many of the duties formerly assigned to the Guardian's Office, such as public relations and legal affairs. The second new corporation, the Religious Technology Center, appeared in 1982. It has ultimate ecclesiastical authority in the church. Through the church's first generation, Hubbard personally owned all of the trademarks and service marks utilized by Scientologists, but these were turned over to the new center which has since controlled the licensing of these items to other church (and non-church) entities.

In spite of the controversy which followed the church through the years, it continued to grow and spread. At the beginning of the 1960s, it had just begun to break out of the English-speaking world. However, from the initial non-English-speaking church in Paris (1959), new churches were founded successively in Denmark (1968), Sweden (1969), and Germany (1970). Through the 1970s, Scientology spread through Europe, with churches being opened in Austria (1971), Holland (1972), Italy (1978), and Switzerland (1978). Groups and missions which would become churches would be found in most of the remaining European nations. Scientology centers could be found in fifty-two countries in 1980. That number had expanded to seventy-four by 1992 and included all of the countries of the former Soviet bloc.

Step-by-step, beginning with his withdrawal from administrative duties, and especially after the removal of the Sea Org to the Flag Land Base in 1975, Hubbard relinquished control of the church to the new generation of leaders. By 1975 most of his research incorporated into the higher OT levels of the church program had been completed, though they would be released to the advanced membership in stages through the remainder of the decade. During the last years of his life, only a small number of close associates had contact with him. He settled first in Florida, but eventually took up residence in rural California in a home outside San Luis Obispo.

During these last years, his consideration of two major social problems led to the development of the church's drug rehabilitation program, the Purification Rundown, and his writing of a concise moral code in response to the perceived decline in public morality, *The Way to Happiness,* which church members have circulated widely. Hubbard also revisited his earlier writing career and celebrated fifty years as a professional writer by authoring a massive science fiction novel, *Battlefield Earth,* which enjoyed good reviews from the genre press. Accompanying the book was an album of music he composed. He followed *Battlefield Earth* with a ten-volume science fiction novel, *Mission Earth,* each volume of which also made the *New York Times* bestseller list.

Hubbard died on 24 January 1986, and has remained as newsworthy in the years since his death as he was during his life.[29] After a suitable pause to acknowledge its founder's life and accomplishments, the church continued its forward march. As a memorial to the founder, each Church of Scientology now maintains an office room, complete with a collection of Hubbard's books, a desk with writing instruments, and a picture of Hubbard, as if one day he might walk into the building and need a place to continue his work.

2.

What Is Dianetics/Scientology?

DIANETICS

Dianetics, as synthesized by Hubbard through the 1940s, began with the assertion that the basic principle of existence is to survive.[1] Each individual possesses an urge to survive that finds expression in the demonstration of positive virtues. Actions toward survival yield pleasure. In like measure, destructive activity leads toward disappointment, failure, pain, and ultimately death. The urge to survive finds expression in various realms—Hubbard termed them dynamics. For example, the individual has a desire to survive as an individual (the first dynamic) as well as to survive through the procreative process and the raising of children (the second dynamic). Each succeeding dynamic envisions a more encompassing arena for activity.

In the everyday life of individuals, the drive to survive is inhibited by aberrations ranging from simple neuroses to different psychotic states to various kinds of sociopathic behavior patterns. Dianetics, the original system defined by Hubbard, outlined a science of the mind that includes an explanation of the source of psychological and social pathology and proposes a therapy system by which they could be totally eradicated. The goal of such therapy would be the production of the optimum individual, the Clear, defined as an individual entirely free of all psychoses, neuroses, compulsions, repressions, and self-generated diseases.

Each individual possesses a mind whose purpose is the solving of problems relative to survival. The mind is motivated toward this end. Thus the question Hubbard attempted to answer became, "Why does the mind frequently dictate actions which are counter-survival?" Hubbard located the distortion in the mind's basic activity of processing data. Moment by moment, the mind receives a mass of data and stores each moment as an image, analogous to a snapshot picture, though that image is really something much more than a picture. It is three-dimensional and contains wide-ranging data on tastes, smells, textures, sounds, etc. The cumulative record of these images recorded moment by moment, called the time track, is likened unto a motion picture film with each frame being the complete image of any given moment.

Hubbard also concluded that the mind had two very important aspects. Most of us are familiar with one part, the analytical mind. That is the aspect of the mind in operation under normal waking consciousness. It takes in data, remembers them, manipulates them (thinks about them), and makes survival-oriented judgments based upon rational considerations. The mind can think at various levels from the concrete to the abstract. It can, for example, recall a particular individual, or imagine a group of people, or even contemplate the totality of humanity. However, less understood are those times when the analytical mind does not function, primarily moments when the individual is partially or fully unconscious. In such moments, which might range from being unconscious on an operating table to the momentary distortion of consciousness induced by the intrusion of great pain, the analytical mind is pushed aside and what is termed the reactive mind takes over. During those times, the reactive mind receives the data and stores them in its own mental data bank.[2]

The images recorded by the reactive mind differ somewhat from those stored in the analytical mind's soundtrack. These particular images, termed engrams, are much more complete and intense; they include a mass of details which the analytical mind might conclude were irrelevant. For example, a man goes into a restaurant for dinner but gets into a fight with another person. He is hit on the head with a chair and falls to the floor unconscious. The assailant spits on the man, and lets out a stream of expletives. The waiter drops the dishes he was carrying, a waitress screams, the owner slams the door to the kitchen. The smell of garlic permeates the air. The total engram would contain all these elements and more.

From such an incident, according to Hubbard, we can begin to see the difference between an engram and ordinary images in our memory bank. The reactive mind thinks in identities. One element of an image is identified or equated with the others. Thus, in the example offered above, the pain of the knockout blow is equated with being spit upon, and is the same as dishes falling or the door slamming or the smell of garlic. Each of those elements equals all the negative things shouted as the man lay on the floor. Each element in the engram equates with each other element.

The practical effect of storing an engram comes in recall. If in the present several of the elements in the engram are again experienced, the entire engram can be brought to the surface. For example, one evening at home the man's wife drops a dish just as their son walks in and slams the door just as someone on the television screams. The engram is re-activated. The man develops a sudden headache and feels a sense of humiliation, but does not know why. The words spoken by the assailant in the past have become labels that stick to the person in the present. The pain and sense of humiliation are experienced but have no logical relation to the events occurring in the present environment. Restimulated several times, an individual engram can lead to various psychological, emotional, and/or psychosomatic illnesses.

Once Hubbard posited the existence of the reactive mind and its engrams, he went about discovering a means of eradicating the effects of the engrams. The counseling technique for calling them up and dealing with them is termed auditing. The counselor, called an auditor, offers directions or asks questions of the person being counseled, called a pre-Clear. As an auditor leads the pre-Clear through a set of related directions or questions (a process), the pre-Clear confronts the engram and learns about some aspect of his/her existence. As one goes through different processes, various engrams are encountered, and through awareness of its existence, the emotional charge can be removed. The power of the engram to affect the individual is taken away.

Hubbard transformed the auditing process into a technology by his discovery, organization, and delineation of the exact sets of directions/questions which most efficiently and effectively lead the individual to the state of Clear. Auditing is further enhanced by the use of the E-meter that allows the auditor to focus upon the engrams; its impersonal movements prevent the pre-Clear from running away from those less attractive aspects of his/her personality.

The E-meter measures the variant strengths of an minute electrical current which is passed through the body of a pre-Clear.[3] As emotional states change, the resistance var-

ies and is immediately indicated on the dial. It is understood by church members that properly used by a trained
auditor, the current fluctuation on the E-meter registers
the changes in mental states, and, most importantly, shows
the changes as an engram is recalled and the emotional
charge attached to it is neutralized.[4] As with any counseling process which surveys a person's entire life, many intimate, embarrassing, and even questionable incidents may
be highlighted. A file of information concerning a person's
past actions which may be compiled as auditing continues
might offer the possibility of misuse. For example, were
the content of a file leaked, it could be used to blackmail an
individual who had disclosed past illegal or immoral acts.
Some former Scientologists have charged that, in fact, such
illicit use of their auditing files has occurred. Going far beyond those reports, some critics have charged that the misuse of auditing files are (or have been) a common practice
within the church in an attempt to control undisciplined
members. Generally speaking, although amid the hundreds
of thousands of hours of auditing done in the church an occasional abuse may have occurred, the charges of abuse
have not been substantiated when presented in courts of
justice, and we are thus left with a lack of verified evidence
of any invasion of members' auditing files or invasion of
their privacy. Such actions would run counter to the basic
rules taught by auditors in their professional code of conduct to which each must adhere. Each auditor promises
"never to use the secrets of a pre-Clear divulged in session
for punishment or personal gain." Any auditor found operating in violation of "The Auditor's Code" would be dismissed from the church's staff.

Progress in Dianetics/Scientology is through a step-by-
step process which includes training classes and auditing.

The entire set of course work and auditing is termed, as mentioned earlier, the Bridge to Total Freedom, and the church provides a detailed chart which describes the route each person follows. Church members view themselves as moving up the bridge, and as they reach each new level, they are presumed to have arrived at a more heightened awareness. At one point along the bridge, the member learns how to audit others and from that time forward spends at least a minimal amount of time assisting those just beginning their training.

FROM DIANETICS TO SCIENTOLOGY

At first glance, there is little in basic Dianetic processing to suggest religion. However, even as Dianetic counseling excited the readers of Hubbard's first book, he turned his attention to the second problem in self-understanding, given the posited truth of Dianetics—the nature of the entity which was viewing the images being processed by the mind. Observations led Hubbard to the conclusion that the essence of the human being was neither the body nor the mind but a third reality, a spiritual being. While this was not a unique conclusion in itself, the nature of the mind which Hubbard had defined dictated to some extent the unique nature of the spiritual being he found. While this spiritual being resembled what others had called the human spirit or soul, he chose to call what he was describing as a thetan. According to Hubbard, the thetan is the person him/herself, that entity which is aware of being aware. One does not have a thetan, one is a thetan.

A key observation which spurred Hubbard's speculation was the phenomenon of exteriorization. In the experience of the thetan leaving and existing consciously apart from the body, the individual comes to know the truth that she or he is not the body but in fact a spiritual being.[5] The experience of exteriorization also suggested that the spiritual being not only could survive apart from the body, but in fact had in the past inhabited other bodies.[6]

The positing of the thetan as the true self allowed a deeper understanding of the dynamics and a more complete explanation of them. In Dianetics four dynamics were described. In Scientology the number was expanded to eight.[7] The thetan as a prime directive is commanded to survive, or, better stated, it is the essential nature of the thetan to survive. As one attains heightened awareness of the self as an individual spiritual being, the drive to survive expresses itself in ever more encompassing circles. First, the individual seeks to survive as an individual, to enjoy the longest, fullest life for the self. The individual then sees survival through procreation or creativity, through the family unit and the next generation. Then successively the thetan seeks survival through groups, the entire human species, and eventually life itself. The sixth, seventh, and eighth dynamics find the individual seeking to survive through identification with the universe, spirituality, and infinity or the Supreme Being. In his discussion of the eight dynamics, Hubbard has approached a traditional Eastern, monistic, mystical view of the universe very closely.

Hubbard grasped the spiritual implications of the eight dynamics as early as 1951 (and hence it is not surprising that the church was founded so soon after the Dianetic movement began). He spent various periods throughout his life in concentrated exploration of the spiritual world he had intuited. Such further research and speculation resulted in the definition of the higher levels of attainment in Scientology, generally referred to as the OT (or operating thetan) levels. The complete religious world view of Scientology is opened to church members in the study accompanying the OT levels, eight of which have been defined. As with the esoteric teachings of other religions, the exact teachings and practices which constitute the substance of these levels are confidential and shared with church members only. However, from what the church has made available, an overall picture can be constructed.[8]

Hubbard's research led him to follow the time tracks of individuals into the past, first to childhood, and eventually to their existence in other embodiments. Thus very early he came to see the thetan as a being who had lived many millennia and been in many bodies. Hubbard eventually led posed the origin of thetans in an unimaginable past measured in billions of years. Along the way the thetans "fell" into the MEST universe of matter, energy, space, and time. Thetans created MEST themselves, but eventually forgot that they were its creators and remained entrapped in it. They also went through several incidents that had the effect of stripping them of their abilities and eventually even the conscious memory of what had occurred. Their continued adventures over the millennia led them to their twentieth-century earthly existence.[9]

Through Dianetic training, individuals learn with some certainty of the reality of themselves as a thetan or spiritual being. They become familiar with their time track and the nature of engrams as images which exist as energy clusters. Having reached the state of Clear, individuals are now ready to learn to operate as a thetan no longer held in bondage by the reactive mind. He or she is now ready to confront the cosmic barriers to complete freedom. In Dianetics one confronts the engrams which have been built up through this life (and some relatively recent past lives). Now, in a post-Clear state, one must deal with the several incidents which occurred in the cosmic past that continue to inhibit the thetan.

In describing the Clear's condition as she or he begins to function as an operating being, Hubbard related an account of cosmic catastrophes through which the race of thetans passed. His account had been characterized by critics of the church as bad science fiction. In fact, his account is much closer to the ancient Hindu myths of creation, multiple universes, and cosmic struggle. The truth of the often fantastic mythology is found in the corresponding realities in the body and consciousness. In their confrontation of the human (i.e., thetan) condition, the individual is aided by a set of disciplines (the technology of auditing) analogous to the more meditative and introspective forms of yoga.

It is not clear how literally Hubbard expected church members to accept the mythology of the OT levels. As with biblical mythology, aspects are difficult to correlate with, for example, modern geological findings. But as is the case with New Age notions of Atlantis and Lemuria, Hubbard may merely have meant this cosmic history to be received as mythological truth, stories which tell the truth about the self better than mere abstract propositions. It is the case, however, that on whatever level Scientologists have received this mythology, they have found it a meaningful tool in their quest to become fully spiritual beings.[10]

ETHICS AND JUSTICE

Just as the church's theology begins with the human urge for survival, so Hubbard began with survival as the starting point for his development of Scientology ethics, which he saw as a rational ethical system,[11] as opposed to the dominant ethical systems of both Eastern and Western religions built on tradition and revelation. Deemed good are those actions which promote survival across the eight dynamics or realms of action. Good actions are constructive, bad actions are destructive. In a manner that echoes John Stuart Mill's utilitarian approach, Hubbard taught that actions which aid the greater number while harming the fewest are good. Thus within Scientology there is a high demand for ethical action as personal and collective survival depend upon it.

To Scientologists, real life from day to day takes place in ambiguous situations in which survival is occurring to a greater or lesser extent. In typical fashion, Hubbard attempted to quantify the conditions in which a person finds him/herself. Each particular situation can be judged in terms of the individual's power to produce survival-oriented results. Through time it is possible to improve any condition. The ethical system proposes a set of steps or formulas which, if followed, will lead to improved conditions. Each church has an Ethics Officer assigned to teach church members how to apply ethics to their own life situations.

Generally, people would have little problem with Scientology ethics; and, in most situations, it promotes the same virtues that more traditional ethical codes emphasize. But in laying out his ethical system, Hubbard also had to confront the reality of unethical action, the existence of which demands some sense of justice, of righting the wrong of destructive actions. Justice exists, he concluded, primarily to protect society. It shields individuals, social structures, and society in general from the destructive actions of antisocial behavior. Like most churches, Scientology developed an internal justice system to deal with unethical actions by church members.

Crucial to understanding the system is Hubbard's belief that punishment is self-defeating, it merely leads the individual to more antisocial behavior. Thus, within Scientology, people involved in destructive behavior are guided first in making restitution to those harmed by their actions and then to take such additional actions as seem necessary to change the present condition to a higher level. Church officials charged with handling counter-survival situations seek initially to determine what has occurred and subsequently to arrive at a solution that is beneficial to all concerned. The most serious situations concern members who are deemed to be committing ongoing destructive actions against the church itself. In the most severe cases, where those found guilty of such actions refuse either to reform or make restitution, expulsion from the church may be the only remedy. It is at this point that Scientology's critics have, however, accused church leaders of acting unethically.

There have been several cases in which a person was expelled and has subsequently become an outspoken critic of the church. Such individuals are held in contempt by church leaders. Rather than simply defend itself, the church sees it as a duty to go on the offensive against any who oppose it. That policy of countering the enemies of Scientology emerged in the 1960s at a time when federal actions appeared to be threatening the church's very existence. Such aggressive policies provided those in the Guardian's Office with what they believed was sufficient rationale for their illegal and otherwise questionable actions. On the other hand, some critics misinterpreted the statements about opponents in church literature, and accused the church of widespread illegal activities—again, accusations ultimately not sustained in court. Complicating the matter was a short-lived policy known as "fair game" which pertained to the treatment of detractors, specifically the refusal to grant them any form of recourse to the ethics and justice codes of the church. This was misinterpreted to signify the church's active persecution of such detractors, and the policy was canceled as a result. At any rate, in the years since the church abandoned the "fair game" policy and disbanded the Guardian's Office, the number of incidents in which so-called dirty tricks or unethical actions have been undertaken by people in any responsible position in the church has almost disappeared.[12]

The changes in the early 1980s, however, have not lessened the church's reputation for aggressively countering those perceived as its enemies. It has repeatedly moved against former members who have turned on the church, those individuals and organizations (such as the Cult Awareness Network) which announced themselves as opponents of the church, and former church leaders who, after leaving the church, established competing facilities to teach their own version of Scientology apart from the church. Following the changes in 1981-82, several former members stole confidential OT documents. Since that time, they have tried to publish these documents considered the most sacred by the church. Through the mid-1990s, they repeatedly posted them on the Internet.

With copies of OT documents circulating internationally, the church called upon government authorities to recover the hard copies and to prevent their further publication. They claimed that the original documents were stolen and that the church owned the copyrights and publishing rights to them. Their attempts to suppress publication have been somewhat hampered by the fact that the documents were dumped into court records and other official records, which eventually become public documents. While being preventing the illicit publication of the OT documents, they have been unable to retrieve copies made from court records or prevent passages from being published in commentaries on the OT processes, though in some cases these materials have been sealed.

The battles between the church and its critics have led to a number of highly publicized court cases. While the church initiated cases in response to instances in which it felt it had been significantly harmed, a sizable portion was not initiated by the church. However, in each the church reacted vigorously and in the process gained an image as an extremely litigious organization.

Through the 1990s, two issues dominated the church's court appearances. First, the church moved against those individuals involved in attempts to publish the OT documents on the Internet. The issue involved many people not otherwise concerned with the church and its critics, as many who believe in the absolute freedom of access to materials on the Internet aligned themselves with the church's critics, while others defended the church's right to protect its copyrights.

In 1994 the first Internet case was filed against former Scientologist Dennis Erlich who had the previous year published OT materials on a bulletin board. A ruling in November 1995 was the first indication that an Internet provider could be held liable if it knowingly allows a copyright infringement to occur. The following year the court upheld an injunction against Arnaldo Lerma for posting the confidential documents. Subsequent to these verdicts, a set of similar judgments was handed down in the United States and several European countries. These cases culminated in the March 1999 settlement with FACTNet, the organization led by Larry Wollersheim which had earlier won a large judgment against the church. FACTNet agreed to return all copyrighted Scientology material in its possession or control, refrain from reproducing any Scientology materials in the future, and pay to the church $1 million should it or its agents break in the future the agreement reached in the settlement. These cases not only broke new ground concerning the application of copyright law to the Internet, but established the church's ownership and right to control what it considers its most holy documents.

As the Internet cases were being adjudicated, the church also moved against the Cult Awareness Network (CAN), the major group advocating action against so-called cults. More than a dozen of the church's members from around the country filed suits against CAN. While none of these actions was successful, through them the church collected intimate details concerning CAN's inner workings. It became obvious that, although it denied it, CAN was actively engaged in referring callers to deprogrammers.[13] Subsequently, Kendrick Moxon, an attorney who had worked on a number of the church's cases, agreed to represent Jason Scott, a member of the United Pentecostal Church who had initiated a lawsuit following his unsuccessful deprogramming. In 1995 Scott won a large judgment against his deprogrammers, and the jury also included CAN in the judgment. The judgment, upheld on appeal, forced CAN into bankruptcy. A coalition of groups, including Scientology, formerly attacked by CAN, pooled their resources and purchased CAN's name. That coaltion now operates the continuing Cult Awareness Network out of offices in Los Angeles. Meanwhile, supporters of the former CAN created a new organization, the Leo J. Ryan Foundation, in 1999.[14]

L. Ron Hubbard, founder of the Scientology religion, in front of the first established British Scientology church, 163 Holland Park Avenue, London, ca. 1963.

An auditing session utilizing the E-meter.

The FLAG Service Organization (occupying the Fort Harrison Hotel) in Clearwater, Florida, where members participate in advanced auditing levels.

The Founding Church of Scientology in Washington, D.C.

The church's Advanced Organization of Los Angeles building, located on L. Ron Hubbard Way.

The church's American Saint Hill Organization building, located directly across the street from the Advanced Organization building.

Church of Scientology Advanced Organization for Europe, located in Copenhagen, Denmark.

The Tokyo Church of Scientology.

The Church of Scientology Celebrity Centre International in Hollywood, California.

Teaching young people right from wrong utilizing *The Way to Happiness*.

Students inspired by *The Way to Happiness* promote the ideal of setting a good example.

A South African drill team promotes *The Way to Happiness*.
(From *ABLE Solutions* magazine.)

Narconon Mediterrano in Spain, one of dozens of Narconon
drug rehabilitation centers around the world.

Scientologist Ann Roberts trains teachers in Zimbabwe utilizing the "Study Technology" developed by L. Ron Hubbard.

Hollywood Education Literacy Project (H.E.L.P.) volunteers tutor young people and adults using the Study Technology.

Russian soldiers are introduced to *The Way of Happiness*.

The original Narconon drug rehabilitation program founded in 1966 by inmate William Benitz (far right) in Arizona State Prison.

Scientologists march for religious freedom in Portland, Oregon, in 1985.

Celebrities join members of the Citizens Commission on Human Rights to demonstrate against the drugging of children with psychiatric mind-altering drugs.

David Miscavige, chair of the Board of Religious Technology Center, the organization established to protect the Scientology religion and maintain the purity and ethical use of its technology.

3.

The Organization of Scientology

What is now the Church of Scientology began as small groups of people gathered to do Dianetic counseling. To this day, the growing edge of Scientology is still found in small Dianetic counseling groups and missions where field auditors introduce people to Scientology and offer basic counseling. Missions, more formally organized than the counseling groups, assist people who are ready to start up the bridge and encourage them to continue their efforts at the nearest local Church of Scientology. Where no groups or missions are readily available, individual field auditors may operate alone. The church supports its field auditors directly through the International Hubbard Ecclesiastical League of Pastors (IHELP), and the missions through Scientology Missions International.

Local churches are prepared to assist members with both the counseling (auditing) and class work that will allow them to reach the state of Clear. They are also the major focus of the church's interaction with the community as they motivate members to become involved in the church's social service and community action programs. The church differs from a mission significantly in that only at the church can those wishing to prepare for the ministry receive the necessary training and ordination. Missions and local churches are autonomous corporations, locally governed following the organizational structure developed by Hubbard. Local churches receive licenses from the Religious Technology Center to use Scientology trademarks and offer specific courses and levels of auditing. Emphasis is placed upon following the spiritual technology to ensure a uniform delivery of training and auditing from church to church. Deviation from the technology provides a rationale for a church's licenses to be revoked.

The Saint Hill Organizations, named for the Saint Hill estate where Hubbard resided for a number of years in the 1960s, function as the colleges for Scientology. Auditors and ministers can go for advanced training and generally attend in blocks of time from three months to a year. Here they receive an overview of Scientology and practical instruction aimed at improving their ability to assist parishioners. Currently, Saint Hill Orgs can be found in Los Angeles, Sydney, Australia, and in England at East Grinstead.

An individual church member who wishes to proceed beyond the state of Clear to become an operating thetan can attend one of the Advanced Organizations, now located in Los Angeles, Sydney, East Grinstead, and Copenhagen, Denmark. The Advanced Organizations provide OT I through OT V auditing/coursework for members and also have facilities to assist auditors with the equivalent of postgraduate training in counseling.

Two unique structures within the Church of Scientology are the Flag Service Organization and the Flag Ship Service Organization, both of which continue the work begun by Hubbard aboard the *Apollo* in the 1970s. While some of the advanced levels which were researched there were transferred to the Advanced Organization, the delivery of the very highest levels of Scientology training have been given over to Flag. The Flag Service Organization, located in Clearwater, Florida, the largest Scientology center in the world (over 750 full-time staff) offers the auditing/course work for OT VI and OT VII as well as a variety of specialized auditing for particular concerns. The Foundation Church of Scientology/Flag Ship Service Organization, which provides the highest level of Scientology training, is currently located aboard the *Freewinds,* a 450-foot ship. Members will generally stay on board the ship in a combined retreat/vacation-like environment where they may receive OT VIII as well as a variety of advanced courses and specialized counseling to enhance OT abilities. The actual content of the course work at both Flag centers is confidential; however, it continues that work provided through the Dianetic and OT training received at a local church and the Advanced Organization.

Since 1981, all of the churches and organizations of the church have been brought together under the Church of Scientology International. SCI provides a visible point of unity and guides the individual churches, especially in the area of applying Hubbard's teaching and technology in a uniform fashion. It also coordinates church growth, and, since its founding, Scientology has been introduced into some twenty-five additional countries and the number of people on the church's staff has more than doubled. Among its unique tasks is that of overseeing the translation of Hubbard's books into different languages.

Operating at the highest ecclesiastical-level structure is the Religious Technology Center. Scientology gives the same attention to the exactness in the application of its spiritual technology that other churches give to orthodoxy. The task of seeing that the technology is uniformly applied and kept at the highest quality possible has been assumed by the Religious Technology Center. At the same time, the center has formal ownership of all Dianetics/Scientology trademarks. The various missions, churches, and organizations, all autonomous corporations which fellowship with the larger movement, receive licenses to use the church's trademarks, service marks, and copyrights of Hubbard's published and unpublished works from RTC. Representatives of RTC regularly visit local churches to verify the quality and preciseness of the teachings being offered to the church's members. The center has the authority to pull the licenses of any church which fails to meet the standards expected of it.

Paralleling the RTC is the Church of Spiritual Technology created in 1982 to receive the bulk of Hubbard's estate, especially his many writings, and to preserve those writings for posterity. The center's staff has copied the writings on the most indestructible of materials and placed them in the most secure containers as a hedge against any possible future catastrophe.

Besides the various centers that constitute the church's organization from the counseling group to the RTC, there are a number of specialized organizations which have been assigned specific tasks. Among the most noteworthy of these are the Celebrity Centers. Over the years, no small part being due to the church's significant presence in the Hollywood section of Los Angeles, a number of celebrities have been attracted to the church. They, like other members, have found the Dianetics training helpful, but additionally have appreciated the church's special efforts to nurture the arts. It is the church's belief that artists can have a special role to play in utilizing their skills to elevate culture, and the church has a special role in assisting artists improve their ability to communicate with the public. Celebrity Centers are equipped to offer all the course work and auditing as local churches of Scientology.

The church also moved in 1984 to unite its worldwide membership in the International Association of Scientologists (IAS) for the specific purpose of ensuring continuation in the spirit of the Creed of the Church of Scientology which calls for equal rights and religious freedom for all people. The catalyst for forming the IAS was the heightened sense of the church being under attack by the combined forces of the anti-cult movement, the courts, and several governments. Over the years of its existence, IAS has been active in keeping the membership informed of religious freedom issues before the church and in honoring Scientologists in the forefront of civil rights efforts.

Within the church there is an ordered community which functions much like the monastic orders in other religions. The Sea Organization includes the most dedicated church workers. Members of the Sea Org sign a contract not only for this life but for future lives. They serve as staff for the Advanced Organizations and for the church's international and continental management.

The church has given a high priority to the publication of Scientology books, the largest percentage of them written by Hubbard. A high percentage of people drawn to the church made their first contact through reading *Dianetics: The Modern Science of Mental Health.* From the original publications organization started by Hubbard in Washington, D.C., three structures have emerged: Bridge Publications in Los Angeles, the Scientology publisher serving North America; New Era Publications in Denmark, serving Europe and the rest of the world; and Golden Era Productions, which produces a wide variety of audio visuals. Responsibility for the non-Scientology writings of Hubbard have been handed over to a separate corporation, Author Services, Inc., which pursues around the world the translation and publication of Hubbard's science fiction, fantasy, and adventure fiction.

SOCIAL BETTERMENT PROGRAMS

Association for Better Living and Education

While the Church of Scientology has been best known for its work with individuals, founder L. Ron Hubbard also projected a vision of the ideal society. Just as Scientology was assisting people in general to rid themselves of the things that inhibited their functioning in day-to-day life, it was perceived that the same training could be targeted to specific problems (drug use, crime, illiteracy) that were not only shared by a large number of people but were undermining the very fabric of society. That insight gave birth to the first of the church's special outreach programs, Narconon. Additionally, beyond his work creating Scientology, Hubbard gave thoughtful attention to various topics (such as education and public morality) which Scientologists see as having general applications far beyond the church. Individual Scientologists have formed special organizations to share Hubbard's wisdom in these specific areas. As the number of independent applications of Hubbard's material multiplied, the Association for Better Living and Education (ABLE) was created in 1988 to coordinate, publicize, and inform church members of the various programs. ABLE also funnels contributions from the church members and public institutions to support social betterment causes.[1]

Narconon/Criminon

Narconon, the oldest of ABLE's social service programs, began with the discovery by William Benitez, an inmate at the Arizona State Penitentiary, of Hubbard's text *Scientology: The Fundamentals of Thought*. An addict since his early teens, Benitez had been unsuccessfully fighting his habit which had landed him in prison on several occasions. Applying Hubbard's ideas, he was finally able to free himself from drugs, and soon concluded that Hubbard's teachings would also be relevant to his fellow prisoners. He was allowed to start a pilot program which he led during the several years left in his sentence. Its initial success won the prison administration's support for its continuance.

Encouraged by his correspondence with Hubbard, after leaving prison in 1970, Benitez settled in Los Angeles and, with the church's help, established a separate non-profit public benefit corporation for the national office for Narconon and initiated programs in other correctional institutions modeled on the one in Arizona. (Public benefit is a category assigned by the state and is evidence that the corporation is not religious, which is another category.) The work soon expanded to include youthful offenders. Then over the next few years, Narconon redirected its efforts toward drug addiction within the general public and opened resident facilities where individuals could finish the entire program in a supportive environment. The largest such Narconon facility is located in Chilocco New Life Center near New- kirk, Oklahoma. Through the 1990s, Narconon International has spread the program to Canada and a number of European countries.[2]

Closely related to Narconon in its scope and purpose is a parallel program in general use among church members, many of whom have previously been drug users or generally suffer from the cumulative effects of the large variety of drugs which now permeate Western society. It was Hubbard's contention that the build up of drugs and other toxins in the body often formed a crucial barrier to spiritual growth. The Purification Program, currently one of the most visible in any Church of Scientology, uses a combination of exercise, saunas, vitamins, and diet to assist the body in eliminating poisons stored in the fatty tissue. This body cleansing effort is then combined with auditing and processing designed to rid the mind of the deleterious effects of the drugs on the mental programming and to redirect the person toward a new healthy lifestyle.

Criminon grew out of the successful experiments of Narconon in the prison system. During the early stages of William Benitez's program at Arizona, a decision was made to open the Narconon program up to all interested inmates whether they were on drugs or not. Among those not on drugs, the emphasis became one of generally cleaning up their lives and preventing their return to prison once released. In the early 1970s, as Narconon began to redirect its work toward the general population, Criminon emerged as the new prison-oriented program which filled the vacuum. Now operating in more than 200 correctional facilities, the program attempts to speak to the loss of self-respect that Hubbard understood to be the source of a person's need to turn to crime. It also deals with some very practical needs of improving literacy, communication skills, and the need to change one's environment upon leaving prison. Because of its positive effects upon those who complete the program, measured in their not returning to a life of crime and prison, Criminon has experienced a steady growth.

Applied Scholastics

Difficulties experienced by church members in reading and mastering the Scientology textbooks alerted Hubbard to deficiencies in the contemporary educational system that often failed to train students in the basic techniques of acquiring new knowledge. In response, he developed manuals on such elementary topics as *How to Learn* and *How to Study*. These materials proved successful in assisting church members in mastering the course work and getting through the massive literature produced by the movement. Then, toward the end of the 1960s, several public school teachers (who were also Scientologists) experimented with Hubbard's educational material in their classrooms and later reported on their students' improvement to church officials. Having concluded that Hubbard's basic approach to education had broad applications quite apart from Scientology, some teachers and educators (who also happened to be church members) established Applied Scholastics to expand the application of the study material in private and public school settings.

Applied Scholastics has worked very quietly for a quarter of a century, during which time it has expanded internationally with affiliates currently functioning across Europe, as well as in Mexico, Australia, Malaysia, China, and South Africa. In the Third World, the program has been used to great effect in equipping those elementary and secondary school teachers who in turn are on the front line attacking the problems of widespread illiteracy. In the United States, Applied Scholastics licenses several successful private schools such as the Delphian School in Oregon and the Ability Plus school in southern California, both now in their third decade of operation. The study program has also been introduced into large corporations as part of the management training program, and, most recently, the growing organization has opened several literacy centers in American cities to teach any who cannot read and study.

The Way to Happiness Foundation

Toward the end of his life, Hubbard considered the problem of the overall moral climate of the modern world. It had been his observation that unlike every successful culture (all of which had produced a set of broad guidelines for the conduct of the individual's life), the modern world had failed to produce a moral code befitting the fast-paced life of the contemporary West. He set himself the task of generating such a code based not on religious presuppositions but common sense and the basic human desire for survival. The results were twenty-one precepts and an accompanying essay, *The Way to Happiness*. He felt the approach could find some consensus across the multicultural situation of the present world.

The Way to Happiness Foundation has overseen the translation of *The Way to Happiness* into a number of languages and coordinates its printing and distribution in mass quantities. It operates primarily through locating sponsors who will underwrite the publication and distribution of the booklet to a specific audience. The foundation has made an effort to get copies into the hands of community influentials both in the United States and around the world and generally met with a favorable response, manifested in the orders for mass quantities to distribute to police officers, soldiers, and students.

SOCIAL REFORM PROGRAMS

Citizens Commission on Human Rights

Few causes are so dear to Scientologists as the church's campaign against psychiatry. Dianetics was originally defined in large part in contrast to various psychological disciplines; and early in his adulthood, Hubbard developed a particular antipathy toward several psychiatric procedures such as electric shock treatment and surgical operations (especially lobotomies) aimed at altering behavior. The Citizens Commission on Human Rights, founded in 1969, has been in the forefront of Scientology's exposure of psychiatric abuse. Over the quarter century of its existence, it has fought to restrict the use of electric shock and lobotomies, campaigned to expose experimental treatments which violated patient rights, lobbied against the use of mood-altering drugs (including but by no means limited to LSD, Valium, Ritalin, and Prozac), and publicized cases of psychiatrists caught in abusive or immoral relationships with patients.

Scientology believes psychiatry is built upon a false foundation which ignores basic insights discovered by Hubbard—that the mind is composed primarily of mental image pictures, that the brain is simply a conduit for the mind, and that humans are essentially spiritual beings. Rather, according to Hubbard, psychiatry and the related field of psychology have built their understanding on the premise that humans are basically animals, that mental activity originates in the brain, and that humans respond most directly to environmental stimuli.

Scientology has also charged that, however well meaning some individual practitioners may be, psychiatry as a field has become permeated with criminality and has repeatedly offered itself as a governmental tool for political suppression. The antipathy between Scientology and psychiatry has taken on an added dimension recently as the main theoreticians of the anti-cult brainwashing perspective are psychiatrists (and psychologists in private practice), a few of whom have repeatedly appeared in court cases as expert witnesses against the church.[3]

In gathering documents concerning the original governmental actions taken against the church in the United States and Australia, leaders have come to feel that the church has been and, to some extent, continues to be the target of an intent to destroy it. They see the opposition voiced by psychiatrists immediately after publication of *Dianetics* and psychiatry's role in the initiating government actions against the church in the 1960s in both Australia and the United States. Beyond the dismissal of Dianetics as pseudoscience, church leaders believe that Scientology became embroiled in the attempts of CIA-funded psychiatrists to find a means of mind control. In fact, a number of psychiatrists, such as UCLA professor Louis J. West, later revealed to have been on the CIA's payroll, subsequently emerged as vocal critics of Scientology.

National Commission on Law Enforcement and Social Justice

Scientologists believe that they have been victimized by false critical information placed in secret government files. In the 1960s, for example, as problems with government agencies in the United States emerged in other countries, church leaders found themselves confronted with accusations that had little to do with the reality of the Church of Scientology as they knew it. Such "information" had its most devastating effect in Australia where for a period the church was actually forced to disband. Hoping to clean government files of such false reports, in 1974 the church founded the National Commission on Law Enforcement and Social Justice (NCLE).

The first major target of NCLE turned out to be Interpol,

the international police organization. The year of its found-ing, the church launched its attack with an initial report charging Interpol with deliberately passing false reports to governments around the world. On occasion these reports led to the subsequent arrest and abuse of innocent individ-uals. Through the next two decades, the church addition-ally charged that Interpol operated without government oversight and continually acted in ways that overrode indi-vidual liberties and human rights. It takes credit for major alterations in U.S. governmental policy towards Interpol. Paralleling the efforts of NCLE, the Church of Scientology has also lobbied for laws which open government files to public scrutiny. To date, such laws (some of them influ-enced by Scientology/NCLE campaigns) have been passed in France, Canada, Australia, New Zealand, Italy, and Bel-gium. The church has also made full use of the Freedom of Information Act in the United States, and has published and widely disseminated a booklet informing the public on using the act to gain access to relevant government files.

WORLD INSTITUTE OF SCIENTOLOGY ENTERPRISES

During the early 1960s, while serving as executive di-rector for the Founding Church of Scientology, Hubbard drafted a model of organization for the local churches of the growing movement. Today his organizational plan, whose structure and operation are detailed in the twelve volumes which comprise the Organizational Executive Course and the Management Series, is used at every level of the church. Business people in the church, having already used Hubbard's writings on group life with some success, began also to see the applicability of Hubbard's organiza-tional materials to their businesses and informally began to write manuals based upon the church's management mate-

rial for training employees. The benefits received from using the material led to the formation of the World Institute
of Scientology Enterprises (WISE) in 1979. The dedicated
Scientologists who currently head the organization believe
that Hubbard's writings can do for group life in general
(and businesses in particular) what Scientology does for
the individual.

WISE operates the Hubbard College of Administration
to train professionals and business people in organizational and management skills using Hubbard's material.
The course covers all aspects of business life and includes a
special emphasis on the development of a heightened ethical environment in the business world.

4.

But Is It a Religion?

With the dawn of the twenty-first century, Scientology has grown into a large international ecclesiastical body with centers in almost half the countries of the world. It has developed a mature theology now readily available in a host of texts and supports a broad program of social service and societal reform. Thousands of people report that the church has given them a satisfying and meaningful spiritual life and perspective. Yet, amid the controversy some people still ask, "Is it a religion?" Given the number of government leaders asking, the question is more than academic, although government policies obviously vary from country to country and are often dictated by local political and religious situations (such as the presence of a dominant religion in some countries).

A large part of the contemporary challenges to the church's religious status comes from those who would place the label "cult" on Scientology. Anti-cultists have attempted to draw a distinction between, on the one hand, religious groups, and on the other, organizations that are distinguished by their utilization of a form of brainwashing (also known as mind control, mental manipulation, or coercive persuasion). According to this approach, cults employ different consciousness-altering techniques that, combined with indoctrination in cult beliefs, lead to the loss of mental freedom among devotees. Attracted to the cult in a moment of weakness, members stay and come to believe the bizarre and baseless teachings because they are quickly subjected to mind control procedures. Such manipulation turns otherwise bright, normal adults into little more than zombies, and prolonged subjugation can cause permanent psychological damage.

This form of brainwashing theory initially arose in the 1950s and was largely discredited by the research done on the returning prisoners of war following the end of hostilities in Korea. It arose again at the end of the 1970s in regard to the spread of new religions in North America and was thoroughly debated by social and psychological scientists through the early 1980s. Again it was unable to survive scrutiny but, nevertheless, has remained popular among critics of Scientology and other minority religions as a means of perpetuating their dislike of different religious bodies.[1]

Although brainwashing rhetoric permeates anti-Scientology literature, quite apart from consideration of mind control or mental manipulation, critics have additionally offered a laundry list of charges against the church and its founder. Assembled together, these additional charges offer a more substantive challenge to Scientology's self-definition as a religion. The first of the initial charges emerged soon after the founding of the Church of Scientology and was central to the attacks on it.

What became Scientology emerged as Dianetics, presented to the world in 1950 as the "modern science of mental health." It was thus introduced to the world as a science dealing with psychosomatic illnesses for which it provided a therapy. As Dianetics swept the country, Hubbard initially turned to the medical and psychiatric establishment for validation. Instead, Dianetics was denounced as medical pseudoscience. In the meantime Dianetics grew as a movement and acquired the E-meter to assist its counseling program.

In spite of rejection by the medical establishment, the movement thrived as people found help through the auditing process. The experiences of people helped by Dianetics provided Hubbard with the necessary validation. The growing movement was, however, radically decentralized, and for a short time Hubbard lost control. Scientology groups began to form as early as 1952, and then in 1954 the first Church of Scientology was founded. Gradually over the next few years, Scientology superseded Dianetics, and churches took the place of Dianetics centers. Critics of the new church, such as the Internal Revenue Service, charged that the founding of the church was purely an expedient step by Hubbard to shield his movement under the special legal protection provided religious groups. It also allegedly allowed him to reassert control of the movement, provided a shield from any claims that he was practicing medicine without a license, and allowed him to pocket the money received for the services provided by the church. Sensing some illegitimacy in Scientology, partially due to hostile appraisals emanating from the mental health community, the IRS began to revoke the tax-exempt status of the individual Scientology churches. It also cited a statement attributed to Hubbard to the effect that anyone who wanted to make millions should found his own religion, an item quoted in most anti-Scientology books but apparently unsubstantiated.[2]

One can have some empathy for the government agents who were looking at the church in the early 1960s. They saw much that simply did not coincide with their own experience of religion. At first sight, the theology of the church appeared to be lacking in references to familiar terms such as prayer, God, faith, etc. Activity was not centered upon weekend worship services, but in mid-week encounters of church members with staff people. And that activity more closely resembled what was occurring in a counselor's office than a pastor's study. Rather than financing the church from voluntary offerings, church members donated a specific amount asked for each activity in which they participated.

Scientologists saw events from a considerably different perspective, anchored in the watershed discoveries made by Hubbard in 1951-52. Originally, they note, Dianetics was indeed modeled as a health delivery service, and its primary benefits described in those terms based on the resolution of psychosomatic illnesses. However, with Hubbard's discovery of the thetan, the spiritual essence of human beings, and the acceptance of past lives,[3] his whole perspective shifted. With this change, for example, auditing still occurred; however, the processing of engrams had shifted its focus away from the body to the thetan. The healing of mind and body, which might still occur, was no longer central; rather, the goal became the rehabilitation of the thetan from all that inhibited its functioning. Additionally, these inhibiting factors were now believed to originate not only in this life, but in the many previous embodiments of the thetan over the past millennia.

In making this shift of perspective, little visibly changed—indeed, even the Dianetic textbooks continue to be used to this day—but the change provided the base upon which Hubbard's mature thought would be built. Although church critics have remained unconvinced of Hubbard's sincerity in making the change, the documenting of the shift two years prior to the founding of the first Church of Scientology has been a key element in the church being able to demonstrate its religious nature in court and before those government agencies that challenged its status.[4]

The accusation that the move from Dianetics to Scientology was purely a matter of expediency was soon expanded into a broad attack upon Hubbard's integrity. For example, the Anderson report challenged the implication that Hubbard's previous training had given him the expertise to make pronouncements in the areas of science. This criticism had been capsulated in the common dismissal of Hubbard as merely a science fiction writer (i.e., a person with a large imagination but little formal education). Other critics, such as former church member Bent Corydon, suggested that the church had so exaggerated and distorted the facts of Hubbard's career as to create a false biography of its founder. He and others have, for example, alleged that Hubbard's knowledge of the Orient was quite superficial, his school record poor, and his World War II service below average. On the latter point, church research has countered the critics' claims by referring to Hubbard's war records and other documents recently recovered through the Freedom of Information Act to which Corydon and others apparently did not have access.

In criticizing Hubbard's early career, critics have also hoped to discount the "research" which served as the foundation upon which Scientology was built. In fact, Hubbard questioned the central role of tradition and revelation as the major sources of authority for religion by adding a third source, science, an authority that has become increasingly popular since the nineteenth century. Like numerous religious teachers of the nineteenth and twentieth centuries, especially in the metaphysical and esoteric realms, Hubbard claimed to base its religious conclusions upon systematic, ordered observation (i.e., research) on the underlying structure of reality. Through the twentieth century, for example, yoga teachers have been most notable for making similar "scientific" claims.[5] In such cases, including Hubbard's, college degrees are ultimately unnecessary, though any experiences or formal training possessed by teachers have been cited as one element contributing to their eventual enlightenment.

In fact, Hubbard never claimed the kind of formal academic credentials which the average scientist or physician possesses, nor did he claim to have done the kind of formal research which would typify standard scientific inquiry in physics or chemistry. Also he made no attempt to publish his research in any recognized scientific journal.[6] His research consisted of the many hours of auditing different people, of his own self-examination, and periods of reflection.

Quite early, Hubbard rejected the scientific establishment and pursued his own observations apart from the general dialogue with colleagues and the received body of knowledge that constitutes science at any given moment.[7] It is also the case that his research led him quickly into metaphysics and speculation about areas beyond the realm of contemporary science. Most scientists would find research concerning past lives and exteriorization, for example, questionable. To the average scientist, claims in these areas belong to the realm of religion. Thus Scientology has found itself in the middle. It has wished to draw upon the image and authority of science, but at the same time the science it professes is grounded in the spiritual realm. In developing an organization to embody and perpetuate such a spiritual science, it has created a church, but one that looks unfamiliar to those used to churches and temples which house other more well-known religious groups built upon ancient traditions or divine revelations. Believers and critics agree: the feeling one receives from a Church of Scientology is completely different from a Christian sanctuary or a Buddhist temple.

One difference between Scientology and the larger, more established churches in the West concerns finances. While most churches raise the money for their operating expenses and mission programs, depending on the country, through either voluntary offerings or (especially in Europe) the receipts from tax revenues, Scientology operates from what it terms the principle of reciprocity. It is the belief of the church that human transactions involve give-and-take and that when members receive the spiritual benefits from the church they should complete the transaction with an act of giving. Normally, that give-and-take involves members donating specific amounts to take a course to receive auditing. It also involves members giving auditing to others or giving of their time and energy to the church.

Critics of the church have suggested that Scientology not only charges for participation in its programs but charges exorbitant fees. Although the costs for the more introductory courses are relatively inexpensive, as one proceeds up the bridge, costs increase, and in the highest levels a course may cost thousands of dollars. As a rule, the great majority of members proceeds up the bridge in a steady rate commensurate with their income. It is, of course, easy to understand that people of other faiths or no faith might question its highly committed members who donate fees for these higher level courses and conclude that these people are throwing their money away. Those who believe that the Church of Scientology teaches worthless material might also feel that it is in effect taking money from people under false pretenses.

The church has countered its critics (including in this case the IRS) by demonstrating that its system of asking for a donation of a specified amount for church services has its analogy in a broad spectrum of churches and religious groups which either have the same system, require members to tithe a tenth of their income, ask specific donations for specific essential services, or otherwise charge for different religious activities. Most recently the Italian Supreme Court agreed with the American IRS that the church's financial system is analogous to the practices of other groups and not out of line with its religious purposes.

However, in a system in which giving and participation in specific activities are so closely tied together, some members have on occasion questioned their financial contributions. Also, given the atmosphere in which members are continually encouraged to hurry up the bridge and to complete their library of church scriptures (Hubbard's writings), a few have claimed that they were talked into acting faster than they would have had they stopped to think about it.[8] Cases have arisen, for example, in which one family member has used family savings for courses despite the disagreement of a spouse, or an enthusiastic member has spent a large sum in an attempt to move up the bridge in a relatively short period. For such occasions, the church has developed a refund policy.

THE FUTURE

The Church of Scientology has experienced four decades of steady growth. While it concurrently overcame one controversy after another, each of which inhibited growth in one country or the other for a brief period, the overall trend within the church has been one of continuous expansion. Internationally hundreds of thousands of people have taken Scientology courses and, if only briefly, affiliated themselves with the church. The church has been among the handful of the many new religions founded since World War II which have successfully spread across the West during the last half of the twentieth century. However, it has emerged at a time of fierce competition by hundreds of groups for the allegiance of the unchurched, a fact which will make it all the more difficult for the church to become a mass movement in the foreseeable future.

The church's immediate future may be affected by the unrelated sentiment generated against minority religions by such tragic incidents as the deaths of members of the Solar Temple. Organized anti-Scientology activity has been evident across Europe since the 1960s. A decade later such activity has become integrated with efforts to counter the growth of the host of new religions which have spread across the continent. German officials have shown a particular antipathy toward the church.

In the wake of the church's expansion into central Europe in the 1970s, an organization devoted especially to opposing the church, Aktion Bildunginformation, began warning the public to avoid Scientology. Taking an activist stance, it filed a series of suits against the church concerning proselytizing in public places, and its book, *The Sect of Scientology and Its Front Organization*,[9] became the first of many German anti-Scientology publications.[10] In 1981 Aktion Bildunginformation founder Ingo Heinemann became the new director of Aktion fur geistige und psychische Freiheit, Arbeitgemein-

schaft der Elterninitiativen e.V. (AGPF), Germany's most
prominent anti-cult organization.

Although many other new religions faced anti-cult sentiment in Germany during the 1990s, Scientology has been
singled out. A problem seems to have emerged in Hamburg
where Scientologists allegedly were attempting to control
the local real estate market. The city established a full-time
office to oppose the church. The present wave of anti-Scientology now moving across the country followed the publication of the first report from Hamburg by the study
group's leader, Ursula Caberta. Over the next few years,
several German government officials declared their opinion that Scientology was not a religion, but merely an economic organization that extracts large fees from vulnerable
members (an opinion contrary to a number of German
court findings in which the issue has been adjudicated).
Subsequently, many regional and local government units
have passed specific measures against the church and its
members. These actions culminated in 1997 with the government announcement that it was placing the church under official surveillance. As early as 1993, the U.S. State Department entered the fray on the church's side, and has
continued to criticize what it sees as the German government's discrimination against Scientology, especially after
the youth organization of the Christian Democratic Union,
Germany's largest political party, instituted boycotts of
films staring Tom Cruise and John Travolta, both well-
known Scientologists.[11] Joined by several human rights organizations, the State Department also noted additional
discrimination in Germany against Jehovah's Witnesses
and several Pentecostal churches. Similar problems were
also noticed in France, Belgium, and Austria, those coun-

tries which have been most open to anti-cult sentiment now evident in Western Europe.

Meanwhile, German courts have not always followed the government's policy, and the Church of Scientology has been able to prevail in a number of important court cases. An important case started in 1986 when a decree of the government of the city of Stuttgart revoked the status of "registered association" of the local mission (called "Association Scientology Neue Brücke"—New Bridge) of the Church of Scientology, claiming that it did not pursue "idealistic purposes" (as "registered associations" do under German law), but rather operated as a commercial undertaking. The suit filed against the decree was originally dismissed by the Administrative Court in Stuttgart, but the State Court of Appeal in Mannheim found in favor of the church and canceled the decree. The Mannheim decision was in turn the subject of a recourse before the Federal Administrative Court. The latter by a decision of 6 November 1997 remanded the case to the State Court, establishing, however, strict guidelines for the remand decision, including the principle that "an idealistic association does not become a business enterprise if it is commercially active in order to accomplish its idealistic purposes."

Scientology's problems in Germany, as disruptive as they are, have been more than balanced by the 1993 resolution of its lengthy battle for recognition with the Internal Revenue Service in the United States. The end of conflict between the church and the United States government, which acknowledged its status as a religion, is destined to have far-reaching influence. The decision follows the opinions of the overwhelming majority of religious scholars and sociologists who have studied the church, a number of whom have been willing to put their opinion in print.

While there will be some continued debate over specific actions taken by the church and its leaders, and over possible definitions of religion, scholars will probably continue in the future to adopt a broad definition, thus including Scientology in a wider religious field. It remains to be seen whether the courts and public authorities will accept this scholarly view, which includes Scientology, or will for their own institutional purposes adopt a more narrow definition that excludes it.[12]

Notes

CHAPTER 1. BIRTH OF A RELIGION

1. Scientology and Dianetics are trademarks of the Religious Technology Center, and the works of L. Ron Hubbard quoted in this work are copyrighted by the L. Ron Hubbard Library.

2. The Church of Scientology has yet to produce a biography of Hubbard, though it has put out a series of biographical booklets which highlight important areas of his life through his own writings and added commentary, and a photographic biography: *L. Ron Hubbard, Images of a Lifetime: A Photographic Biography* (Los Angeles: Bridge Publications, 1996). A comprehensive biography is due out soon. The best of the several biographies attempted by critics, *The Bare-Faced Messiah,* by Russell Miller (New York: Henry Holt, 1988), is seriously lacking as Miller did not have access to many of the documents relating to the rise and progress of the church.

3. On the 70th anniversary of Hubbard's becoming a blood brother, a ceremony commemorating that event was held among the members of the contemporary Blackfoot tribe. Cf. Letter from C. Emerson Fisher, 27 Aug. 1985, copy in the American Religions Collection, Davidson Library, University of California-Santa Barbara, Santa Barbara, California.

4. Indicative of the continuing relationship between Thompson and Freud is an interesting postcard found in the Freud papers at the Library of Congress in which Thompson is thanked for sending his mentor a "charming photograph of the 3 beauties at the Pacific Ocean." Postcard from Sigmund Freud to Thompson, 27 July 1923, in Library of Congress; copy in the

American Religions Collection of the University of California, Santa Barbara.

5. In 1970 an officer of The Explorers Club wrote of Hubbard, "His extensive experience in aerial mapping by camera under almost every type of condition was one of the many qualifying factors for membership. To his credit is the first complete mineralogical survey of Puerto Rico in 1932 and 1933; survey flights throughout the U.S. to assist in the adjustment of field and facility data; Caribbean Expedition resulting in valued data for the Hydrographic Office and the University of Michigan. In 1940 he went to Alaska to rewrite *U. S. Coast Pilot, Alaska, Part 1*, and to investigate a new method of radio-positioning entailing a new aerial and a new mathematical computation and instrument." Letter from Marie E. Roy, 4 Feb. 1970, copy in the American Religions Collection, Davidson Library, University of California, Santa Barbara.

6. Hubbard left the service in February 1946 with twenty-one citations, letters of commendation, and medals on his record. It should be noted that the details of Hubbard's naval career have been called into question by the critics of the Church of Scientology. Critics rely on an alleged copy of Hubbard's notice of separation deposited at the Veteran's Administration and accessible through the Freedom of Information Act. This copy, inter alia, mentions four medals and awards rather than twenty-one. The church has replied by filing in a number of court cases both the original notice of separation kept in the church's archives and expert evidence by military specialists explaining why discrepancies may occur for a number of reasons between an original notice of separation and the copy kept by the Veteran's Administration, insisting that the original should prevail.

7. Along with the assistance he offered to some of his fellow patients at Oak Knoll, Hubbard saw two prior events as forming the trajectory that led to Dianetics. While in college, he became curious about the nature of poetry and wondered why poetry affected us differently than prose writing. Of interest were not so much his results as the method he adopted to answer his question. He used a Koenig photometer (which shows the vocal patterns when held against the diaphragm) and produced graphs of

the two kinds of vibration patterns. He then posed the question of how the mind might respond to different patterns. Second, in 1938 he authored an essay, "Excalibur," which concluded with what became a basic Dianetics/Scientology insight that all life is directed toward survival.

8. Space does not allow a detailed discussion of Hubbard's involvement with the Agape Lodge. I have included a more detailed discussion in the most recent editions of the *Encyclopedia of American Religion* (Detroit Gale Research, 1996), 162, and in my paper published as "Thelemic Magic in America: The Emergence of an Alternative Religion," in Joseph H. Fichter, ed., *Alternatives to American Mainline Churches* (Barrytown, NY: Unification Theological Seminary, 1983), 67-87.

9. In an off-the-cuff remark during the Philadelphia Lectures in 1952 (PDC Lecture 18), Hubbard referred to "my friend Aleister Crowley." This reference would have to be one of literary allusion, as Crowley and Hubbard never met. He obviously had read some of Crowley's writings and makes reference to one of the more famous passages in Crowley's vast writings and his idea that the essence of the magical act was the intention with which it was accomplished. Crowley went on to illustrate magic with a mundane example, an author's intention in writing a book.

10. Critics of the church have gone into great detail to point out possible sources for the various aspects of the teachings of Dianetics and Scientology, and there are certainly numerous points of convergence between Hubbard's teachings and individual ideas and practices available elsewhere. At present, it is not known which aspects of Dianetics Hubbard actually encountered in previously existing sources and subsequently incorporated them into his system and which parts occurred to him independently. The essence of Hubbard's originality, however, lies not so much in the sources of the individual elements as in the synthesizing of them into a finished system.

11. *The Original Thesis* is currently available under the title, *The Dynamics of Life* (Los Angeles: Bridge Publications, 1983).

12. The article, "Dianetics: The Evolution of a Science," appeared in the May 1950 issue of *Astounding Science Fiction,* and

editor Campbell was for several years a major supporter of Hubbard's new approach to mental health.

13. L. Ron Hubbard, *Dianetics: The Modern Science of Mental Health. A Handbook of Dianetic Therapy* (New York: Hermitage House, 1950).

14. (Los Angeles: Bridge Publications, 1989).

15. (Los Angeles: Bridge Publications, 1982).

16. The E-meter has frequently been compared to a lie detector, but such a comparison is misleading. Their only common denominator is a Wheatstone bridge, but the two instruments are designed for completely different purposes.

17. See the discussion of the board's inner turmoil in chapter nine of Hubbard's early work, *Science of Survival* (Los Angeles: Bridge Publications, 1989), 74 (first edition, Wichita, KS: The Hubbard Dianetic Foundation, 1951).

18. Winter had written the preface to the original edition of *Dianetics* and then penned an early favorable account of Hubbard's work, *A Doctor's Report on Dianetics, Theory and Therapy* (New York: Julian Press, 1951).

19. In 1954, through the *Professional Auditor's Bulletin*, Hubbard issued a most enlightening statement on the foundation of the Church of Scientology, the existence of which he had to explain against the criticisms of some of the students of Dianetics. See "Why Doctor of Divinity," *Professional Auditor's Bulletin* 32 (7 Aug. 1954).

20. Hubbard later opined about his offer of Dianetics, "The AMA simply wrote me, 'Why?' and the APA replied, 'If it amounts to anything I am sure we will hear of it in a couple of years.'" Quoted in *Ron The Philosopher: The Rediscovery of the Human Soul* (Los Angeles: L. Ron Hubbard Library, 1996), 14-15.

21. A similar report was prepared in New Zealand though with less hostile conclusions and no recommendations for legislative action.

22. For a discussion of the Scientology situation in Australia, see *Discrimination and Religious Conviction* (Sydney: New South Wales Anti-Discrimination Board, 1984).

23. In 1978 in France, four Scientologists (three, including Hubbard, in absentia) were tried and convicted for fraud. The

conviction was reversed on appeal in one of the French deci-
sions where Scientology was pronounced "religious." French
anti-cult movements, however, continued their attacks against
the church. The substance of their criticism was later incorporated into the French parliamentary report, *Les Sectes en France*
(Paris: Les Documents d'information de l'Assemblé Nationale,
1996). For a scholarly criticism of this report, see Massimo
Introvigne and J. G. Melton, eds., *Pour en finir avec les sectes: le
débat sur le rapport de la commission parlementaire* (3eme ed.,
Paris: Dervy, 1996). This book includes a detailed critical discussion of the report's comments about Scientology by British
sociologist Bryan Wilson ("La Scientologie et le rapport," ibid.,
277-87).

24. George Malko, *Scientology, the Now Religion* (New York:
Delacorte Press, 1970); Paulette Cooper, *The Scandal of Scientology* (New York: Tower, 1971); Robert Kaufmann, *Inside Scientology* (London: Olympia Press, 1972).

25. Omar Garrison, *The Hidden History of Scientology* (London:
Arlington Books,1974).

26. His withdrawal from immediate administrative concerns,
an act quite common among founders of religious groups, has
been viewed by critics as merely a convenient way to shield himself from what they hoped would be definitive actions to be
taken by the government and/or courts against the church. Such
actions, of course, did not occur.

27. The materials and teachings for the Operating Thetan levels of Scientology are considered confidential. They are dis-
cussed only in the most general of terms in the literature and by
the leadership of the church when talking to nonmembers. At
the same time, they have become the subject of a massive controversy. Over the past twenty years, several members who had access to the higher level materials have left the church and stolen
the materials. These former members have tried in various ways
to harm the church by circulating copies of these materials. At
the same time, fake documents purporting to be OT level material have also been produced and circulated. In response, the
church has taken a variety of legal steps to prevent the publication of these claiming copyright ownership.

28. Several people, formerly in the church and negatively affected by the reorganization, left the church at this time and
joined the ranks of its critics. Chief among these was Jon Atack,
author of *A Piece of Blue Sky* and at the center of an anti-Scientology network in the United Kingdom. As might be expected,
those most affected for good or ill by the changes in 1980-81
view what occurred in a very different light.

29. Several years earlier his estranged son had filed a lawsuit
claiming that his reclusive father was already dead and that the
church leadership was concealing the fact. Rather than appear in
court, Hubbard submitted a letter to prove that he was still very
much alive.

CHAPTER 2. WHAT IS DIANETICS/SCIENTOLOGY?

1. As mentioned earlier, Hubbard expressed his basic notion
concerning survival in a 1938 essay, "Excalibur," most recently
reprinted in *Ron The Philosopher.*

2. Students of New Thought metaphysics will see in Hubbard's understanding of the mind some convergence with the
approach of metaphysician Thomas Troward (1847-1916) and
Ernest Holmes (1887-1960), founder of Religious Science, who
proposed a two-layered mind which acted in conscious and unconscious states. For Troward, the two aspects of mind were primarily distinguished by the type of logic (deductive or induc-
tive) they employed. Cf. Thomas Troward, *The Edinburgh Lectures on Mental Science* (London: Stead, Danby and Co., 1904).

3. Possibly the best description of the operation of the E-meter
is found in the report of Canadian engineer Roy E. Dowswell,
Theoretical and Actual Operation of the Electropsychometer (privately published, undated). A copy may be found in the American Religions Collection of the Davidson Library at the University of California, Santa Barbara.

4. It is the use of the E-meter as an essential element in auditing which helped open Hubbard to charges that he was a pur-
veyor of pseudoscience. Critics have belittled the E-meter as
merely a galvanometer, and have noted that all of the effects produced during an auditing session have explanations without the

necessity of any reference to engrams. They also point to the lack of quantified research of the kind generally necessary to back up the claims made for similar instruments. See, for example, the discussion of the E-Meter by Stewart Lamont in *Religion Inc., The Church of Scientology* (London: Harrap, 1986). Scientologists generally respond to critics by affirming the spiritual aspects of Hubbard's research and redirect considerations to the many satisfied church members who have found auditing a means of meaningful self-discovery.

5. The experience of exteriorization is like what is described in the literature of psychical research as astral travel or out-of-body travel. See, for example, the work of Susan Blackmore, *Beyond the Body: An Investigation of Out-of-Body Experiences* (London: Heinemann, 1981), or Robert A. Monroe, *Journeys Out of the Body* (Garden City, NY: Doubleday, 1971).

6. It is to be remembered that Hubbard was beginning his exploration of the life and nature of the thetan in the 1950s at a time when only a few Theosophists made a public profession of belief in reincarnation.

7. In a passing remark in a 1952 lecture, "E-Meter Demo" *(Philadelphia Doctorate Course,* Vol. I, Dec. 1952), Hubbard mentioned the possibility of a 9th dynamic "which would be aesthetics" and of a 10th dynamic "which would probably be ethics." The idea was not further developed and the official teachings of Scientology include only eight dynamics.

8. The Church of Scientology is structured like many esoteric groups on an initiatory degree model. After members have reached the state of Clear, they are invited to successive levels of spiritual knowledge and attainment, each of which is seen to build upon the one before it. Thus, for example, until one satisfactorily completes the work for OT III, the member is not considered spiritually ready to encounter the next level and the material for OT IV is not made available.

The confidential nature of this teaching material has become the object of intense controversy, as several former members who were privy to them left the church. As mentioned earlier, they stole copies and spread them to others. In spite of the church's demand that such material is owned by the church as part of its sacred literature and hence any copies in the hands of nonmembers constitutes stolen property, hostile former members have repeatedly attempted to breach the confidentiality of the church and place copies of the OT material into places accessible to the general public. Copies have been placed in court records and in various public archives, and circulated informally.

Most recently, attempts have been made, with mixed success, to place the documents on the Internet. The church's attempts to stop publication of this material have forced the making of new case law and generated a heated debate over the nature of copyrights, publishing rights, fair comment, and censorship on the Internet.

9. To date Scientologists have not produced the equivalent of a systematic theology. Those with some knowledge of Western thought, however, will immediately recognize its resemblance to Gnostic views and see themes common to the Western esoteric spiritual tradition. Hubbard composed an abstract mythical picture of creation in a brief document, "The Factors," reproduced in *Scientology: Theology & Practice of a Contemporary Religion* (Los Angeles: Bridge Publications, 1998), and also published a small volume, *The Factors* (Los Angeles: Bridge Publications, 1990).

10. Critics of Scientology have attacked the OT levels as an unbelievable myth which no rational, thinking person can believe. A similar attack has been made during the last two centuries by critics of Christianity upon the biblical accounts of the Garden of Eden, Flood, and miracles. To the unbeliever, it is almost always the case that the mythical elements of various religions appear irrational and ridiculous. It is also the case that many people have examined the criticisms leveled at their faith and continue to find meaning and value in its mythological underpinnings.

11. The ethical system of Scientology is based on Hubbard's *Introduction to Scientology Ethics* (Los Angeles: The American St. Hill Organization, 1970). More recently the church has prepared a study course for church members based on the book.

12. The practice of declaring people "fair game" was formally abandoned in 1968, two years after it was instituted. Cf. HCO Policy Letter of 21 Oct. 1968. A comprehensive investigation of

"fair game" accusations was included in the Internal Revenue Service investigation, and satisfying itself that there was nothing to them was an important part of the agency's reaching a final decision on the church.

13. Deprogramming is an anti-cult practice based on the brainwashing hypothesis. Normally hired by concerned parents, deprogrammers kidnap members of new religious movements, keep them in imprisonment, and try to "persuade" them to leave their movements through a variety of techniques, often involving the actual use of violence. From many years forcible deprogramming has been regarded as a criminal offense by courts in the U.S. and elsewhere.

14. In April 1998 the United States District Court of Appeals for the Ninth Circuit upheld the judgment against the Cult Awareness Network and the several individuals responsible for the deprogramming attempt on Jason Scott. Shortly thereafter, the U.S. Supreme Court refused further review of the case. The Scott case appears to have stopped the practice of deprogramming in North America and imposes a formidable obstacle to the new Ryan Foundation's picking up the programs of the former Cult Awareness Network.

CHAPTER 3. THE ORGANIZATION OF SCIENTOLOGY

1. As each program is licensed to use specific, secularized materials written by Hubbard, it is ABLE's task to ensure that each program keeps to its particular mission and does not wander into other areas. Most importantly, the work of the various organizations is clearly separated from the work of the local Scientology churches that are assigned the task of spreading the teachings of Scientology, holding classes in Dianetics/ Scientology for new and perspective church members, and offering counseling (auditing) to church members. Leaders also emphasize that while money from Scientologists flows into ABLE, no ABLE funds flow back into the church.

2. While generally well received in North America, European critics have charged that Narconon is a worthless treatment for which excessively expensive fees may be charged. It has been a

central feature of the Italian court case in Milan. On the other hand, it has been recognized as an effective treatment program in Sweden and Holland.

3. Psychiatrists who have assisted anti-cult activists do not necessarily represent the majority within the mental health professions. In 1987, for example, the Bureau for Social and Ethical Responsibility of the American Psychological Association (APA) rejected, citing "lack of scientific rigor," a report supporting the anti-cult mind control theories as applied to new religious movements. This rejection had far-reaching consequences in U.S. case law.

CHAPTER 4. BUT IS IT RELIGION?

1. Space does not allow a full discussion of the rise and fall of the brainwashing controversy. Among the better surveys of the arguments, see Thomas Robbins and Dick Anthony, "The Limits of 'Coercive Persuasion' as an Explanation for Conversion to Authoritarian Sects," *Political Psychology,* Summer 1980, 22-37; and Dick Anthony, "Religious Movements and 'Brainwashing' Litigation: Evaluating Key Testimony," in *In Gods We Trust: New Patterns of Religious Pluralism in America* (New Brunswick, NJ: Transaction Books, 1989).

2. There is no record of Hubbard having ever made this statement, though several of his science fiction colleagues have noted the broaching of the subject on one of their informal conversations. The actual quote seems to have come from a cynical remark in a letter written by Orwell published in *The Collected Essays, Journalism, and Letters of George Orwell,* edited by Sonia Orwell and Ian Angus (New York: Harcourt, Brace and World, 1968), 304.

3. Church members avoid the use of the more common term reincarnation as they wish to make it clear that they do not accept the idea of transmigration, that is, that a thetan could ever reincarnate as a less than human species.

4. Among those who emerged as most doubtful on this question was Kevin Victor Anderson, who authored the lengthy anti-Scientology report that led to the church's being banned in parts

of Australia for almost two decades. See especially chapter 10 of his report of the *Board of Inquiry into Scientology* (Australia: State of Victoria, 1965). When finally tested in court, Anderson's arguments did not stand.

5. For example, see Swami Brahmavidya, *Transcendent Science; or, The Science of Self-Knowledge* (Chicago: Transcendent Science Society, 1922); Gopi Krishna, *The Biological Basis of Religion and Genius* (New York: Harper & Row, 1972); or Maharishi Mahesh Yogi, *The Science of Being and Art of Living* (London: International SRM Publications, 1966).

6. It is the case that some of the biographical sketches of Hubbard published by the Church of Scientology contained mistakes and implied credentials for Hubbard which he did not possess (and had never claimed). In its most recent publication, it has moved to correct those errors.

7. Hubbard also joined other religious leaders who had criticized contemporary science for having not only "produced weapons for the annihilation of men, women, and children in wholesale lots" and aided and abetted "Godless totalitarian governments," but for having led humanity "away from the affirmation of the existence of a Supreme Being" and brought man "into a machine-like state." Cf. L. Ron Hubbard, *Science of Survival* (Los Angeles: Publications Organization, 1951, 1975).

8. One set of stories told by disgruntled ex-members of Scientology relates encounters with overly aggressive members who attempted either to convince people to take further courses or encourage them to return to the church after they had left it. As a whole, such encounters appear to be atypical. The overwhelming majority of former members has not reported any harassment following their leaving the church.

9. *Die Scientology-Sekte und ihre Tarnorganisationen* (Stuttgart, 1979).

10. Typical of recent anti-Scientology books are Renate Hartwig, *Scientology: Das Komplott und die Kumpane* (Dusseldorf: Metropolitan Verlag, 1995); Hansjerg Hemminger, *Scientology: Die Kult der Macht* (Stuttgart: Quell, 1997); and Tom Voltz, *Scientology und (k)ein Ende* (Solothurn: Walter-Verlag, 1995).

11. The Church of Scientology has published a number of booklets responding to the situation in Germany, the most informative being *Religious Apartheid 1996: Official Repression of Religious Rights in Germany* (Los Angeles: Freedom Publishing, 1996).

12. In October 1997, in a ruling of particular importance for Europe, the Italian Supreme Court addressed the issue of Scientology's religious status. For the second time, the Court annulled "with remand" a decision of the Court of the Appeal of Milan. This means that there will be an additional future decision from Milan. However, the Supreme Court included one of the most important discussions to date—and on an international scale—of how courts may apply existing laws apparently requiring them to decide if a specific group is, or is not, a religion. Also, in reaching its favorable decision, it considered five major objections to Scientology's religious status raised by the church's critics:

First, critics objected that Scientology is "syncretistic" and did not propose any really "original belief." This is, the Supreme Court argues, irrelevant, since syncretism "is not rare" among genuine religions, and many recently established Christian denominations exhibit very few "original features" when compared to older denominations.

Second, it has been argued that Scientology is presented to perspective converts as science, not as religion. The Supreme Court replied that, at least since Thomas Aquinas, Christian theology has claimed to be a science. On the other hand, science claiming to lead to non-empirical results such as "a knowledge of God" (or "of human beings as gods") may be both "bad science" and "inherently religious."

Third, ex-members have claimed that Scientology is not a religion but only a facade to hide criminal activities. The Supreme Court asks how we may know that the opinion of disgruntled ex-members is representative of the larger population of ex-members. Other ex-members have in fact appeared as witnesses for the defense, and, at any rate, the number of ex-members of Scientology appears to be quite large. The opinion of two and even twenty of them, thus, is hardly representative of what the average ex-member believes.

Fourth, texts by L. Ron Hubbard and early Italian leaders seem to imply that Scientology's basic aim is to make money. Such interest in money is, according to the Supreme Court, "excessive" but "perhaps appears much less excessive if we consider how money was raised in the past by the Roman Catholic Church," for example, the late Medieval controversies about the sale of indulgences, or the fact that until very recently Italian Catholic churches used to affix at the church's door "a list of services offered [Masses and similar] with the corresponding costs." The Supreme Court also concluded that *quid pro quo* services are more widespread among religions than the judges in Milan (where this case had originated) seemed to believe.

The court went on to observe that the more "disturbing" texts on money by Hubbard are but a minimal part of his enormous literary production (including "about 8,000 works"); and that they were mostly circular letters or bulletins intended "for the officers in charge of finances and the economic structure, not for the average member." Finally, even if one should take at face value the "crude" comment included in a technical bulletin of Scientology (not written by Hubbard) that "the only reason why LRH [L. Ron Hubbard] established the church was in order to sell and deliver Dianetics and Scientology," this would not mean, according to the Supreme Court, that Scientology is not a religion. What is, in fact, the ultimate aim of "selling Dianetics and Scientology"? There is no evidence, the Supreme Court suggests, that such "sales" are only organized in order to assure the personal welfare of the leaders. If they are intended as a proselytization tool, then making money is only an intermediate aim. The ultimate aim is "proselytization," and this aim "could hardly be more typical of a religion," even if "according to the strategy of the founder [Hubbard], new converts are sought and organized through the sale and delivery of Dianetics and Scientology."

Fifth, the Supreme Court considered the argument that Scientology is not a religion since there is evidence, in the Milan case itself, that a number of Scientologists were guilty of "fraudulent sales techniques" or abused of particularly weak customers when "selling" Dianetics or Scientology. Such illegal activities should be prosecuted, but, the court added, there is no evidence that they are more than "occasional deviant activities" of a certain number of leaders and members within the Milan branch, "with no general significance" concerning the nature of Scientology in general.

Selected Bibliography

Overwhelmingly, books on Scientology have been either publications by the church expounding and defending its position or attacks by its critics. Sociologist Roy Wallis's book, *The Road to Total Freedom* (New York: Columbia University Press, 1977), possibly comes close to a balanced analysis, though church members still find it objectionable.

Essential Church of Scientology publications include the following books by L. Ron Hubbard: *Dianetics: The Modern Science of Mental Health* (New York: Hermitage Press, 1950; reprinted: Los Angeles: Bridge Publications, 1985), 512 pp.; *Fundamentals of Thought* (Los Angeles: Bridge Publications, 1988), 229 pp; *New Slant on Life* (Los Angeles: Bridge Publications, 1988), 206 pp.; *Self Analysis* (Los Angeles: Bridge Publications, 1989), 306 pp. *The Scientology Handbook* (Los Angeles: Bridge Publications, 1994), 871 pp., is a summary of church teachings on a wide variety of subjects. *What is Scientology?* (Los Angeles: Bridge Publications, rev. ed., 1998), 835 pp., is a comprehensive survey of the church's life and thought, and a necessary publication for anyone interested in the church's own self-understanding. Also very helpful is *Scientology: Theology & Practice of a Contemporary Religion* (Los Angeles: Bridge Publications, 1998), 287 pp., that includes reports by several European and American scholars concerning Scientology as a new religion. A long-awaited biography of Hubbard is expected to be published by the church in the near future.

Of volumes published by the church's critics, Stewart Lamont's *Religions Inc.* (London: Harrap, 1986), 192 pp., and Russell Miller's *Bare-Faced Messiah* (New York: Henry Holt, 1987), 390 pp., are by far the best, though the church has prepared statements on each indicating factual errors and omissions. The critical literature, while concentrating on documents less favorable to Hubbard and Scientology, is weakened by its lack of access to the many pertinent documents housed in the church's archives.

About the Series Editor

Massimo Introvigne was born in Rome and is the managing director of the Center for Studies on New Religions (CESNUR), a network of international academic organizations devoted to the study of emerging religious/spiritual movements. An attorney in private practice in Torino, Italy, he has taught courses and seminars in several academic institutions on the sociology and history of new religions. Additionally, he is the author or editor of some forty books and numerous articles and chapters on the same topic.